NEVER
EVER
GIVE UP!

Endorsements

"Patricia did an extraordinary job creating a book for every woman ready to claim her power and step further into her greatness! These pages guide you to what is possible and achievable and what will catalyze you to create a life you absolutely love!"
—Lisa Nichols
CEO, Founder
Motivating the Masses

"In this life-changing book, you will learn to discover and declare your dream life and identify exactly what holds you back from creating the results you desire. If you want a proven blueprint for how to create success in every area of your life, read this book."
—Mathew Boggs
Best-Selling Author
Co-Founder of Brave Thinking Institute

"An award-winning coach, Patricia helps women discover the steps to move their lives from stuck to unstoppable. Her book *Never Ever Give Up!* is an essential guidebook on the path to creating a life you absolutely love!"
—Kirsten Welles
Master Coach
Brave Thinking Institute

"This book will touch your heart and inspire you to be your greatest self. If you know that there is more to create and more to live, but for whatever reason, have felt held back by the stories of your past, get ready for Patricia's book to inspire your transformation. This collection of stories, insights, and keys for real change will help you in practical ways to tap into the life you know you are meant to be living."
—Alina Frank and Craig Weiner, DC
Directors of the EFT Tapping Training Institute and the film, The Science of Tapping *(Craig Weiner and Suzanne Fageol are the co-creators of Tapping Out of Trauma)*

NEVER EVER GIVE UP!

8 Keys to Creating a Life You Absolutely Love©

Patricia Campbell

Goodyear, Arizona

First published in the USA in 2022 by Patricia Campbell

Paperback ISBN: 978-1-958405-32-1
Hardcover ISBN: 978-1-958405-33-8
eBook ISBN: 978-1-958405-31-4

Publishing House: Spotlight Publishing House™ in Goodyear, AZ
Developmental Editor: Dawn Campbell, D-Tales and Redz Writing Hood
Senior Editor: Lynn Thompson, Living on Purpose Communications
Contributing Editor: Colin Campbell
Book Cover: Spotlight Publishing House
https://spotlightpublishinghouse.com
Interior Design: Marigold2k

For information, contact: www.patriciacampbell.ca

DISCLAIMER
The author does not intend the material in this book to be a substitute for trained medical or psychological advice. Therefore, please consult with a professional to treat mental and physical illness. The publisher, author, and the author's team assume no liability for injury caused to the reader that may result from the content contained herein.

All names referenced in this book are used with permission.

Dedication

To my beloved children,
Todd and Di (Dawn), and
my grandchildren, Traimin and Taryn,
the moment each of you was born,
you enriched my life, forever changing me
in the most glorious way. I am eternally grateful
to you and my husband Colin for teaching me to
laugh more often, love more deeply,
and live more richly.

I love you all!

Contents

Acknowledgments   xi
Foreword   xv

Preface – My Story   1
Introduction – Master Your Results   23
Key #1 – Pay Attention to Your Thoughts   31
Key #2 – Design Your Dream Life   39
Key #3 – Courageously Decide   47
Key #4 – Burning Desire   55
Key #5 – Bridge the Gap   69
Key #6 – Befriend Your Fear   81
Key #7 – Break Through Invisible Barriers   103
Key #8 – The Power of Love   125

Bibliography   141
About the Author   145

Acknowledgments

I would like to acknowledge my writing coach, Junie Swadron. You believed in me and this unwritten book from the moment I joined you in your brilliant author mentorship program. Without you, this book would still be just a dream, an unsung song inside me. Thank you for your loving guidance, unwavering support when my paradigms spoke up, and wise suggestions throughout the writing of this book.

To my gifted daughter and developmental editor, Di (Dawn), you took my disjointed stream of thoughts and transformed them into an eloquent flow of stories and, in the end, a book. There are many portions of this book where you were my co-author, and your spirited revisions brought life to the words that helped create a masterpiece. From the bottom of my heart, thank you for your courage in helping me rewrite some of the more personal and painful memories and for bravely sharing your own. Most of all, I am grateful for your genius in hearing the cadence and flow of these words and stories. Dawn Campbell, may your passion and talent for the written word continue to grow and your writing and editing business, D-Tales (Redz Writing Hood), flourish!

To Lynn Thompson of Living on Purpose Communications, senior editor and proofreader, I am eternally grateful for your willingness to do what it took to get this book polished and ready for publication. Thank you for your insightful questions and the depth you went to understand who I am and the message I am committed to conveying so that it makes the difference I feel called to make. You are a rare gem and a dedicated, first-class editor, clearly living your purpose. It is my honor to have your brilliance shine in my life's work.

To Colin, my husband, I am deeply grateful for your immense support with this book. For the many hours you read the pages together with me and helped me find a better word or phrase (your university degree has blessed me). I appreciate you also for all the ways you took care of everything I had no time for—apart from this book. For thirty years, you have lived many of these pages with me through thick and thin, and never once did you waver from your commitment to ensuring our security and financial freedom. Your famous words are etched forever in my being: "Save every receipt, so you know where your money goes." And that is a rich legacy I pray will live on for generations.

To all the beautiful women and extraordinary men (you know who you are) who have supported, loved, taught, and empowered me over the many years of my journey. It would be impossible to list all of you here; know that you are in my heart, and I am eternally grateful for you.

Brenda Jungwirth, my long-time power partner and soul sister, I am eternally grateful for your committed support and for always believing in me and my dreams. It is my honor to partner with you in creating the Women In Dentistry Mastermind. I am inspired by your passion for supporting women to be successful.

Bobbie-Jo Van Ruskenveld, thank you for your dedicated support to women in dentistry. The stories I share from the amazing dentists whose lives you impacted are a testament to your love for your clients and your commitment to superior service.

To Glenis Holmes, my beloved friend and RV partner, for all the ways you helped me be free—with healing, dancing on the beach on the Oregon Coast, and supporting my life's expansion.

To Becky Norwood, my publisher, thank you for your dedication, wisdom, and perseverance in this book becoming a BESTSELLER! I knew from the moment I heard you talk about your passion for publishing books that made a difference that I was meant to work with your publishing company, Spotlight Publishing House.

To my clients, thank you for the honor of trusting me to serve and support you in realizing your dreams.

Because of each of you, I am the woman I am today.

With love and light,
Patricia

Foreword

Was there ever a time in your life when you knew that if you continued on the path you were on, nothing good would come of it? Did that realization lead you to make a non-negotiable pact with yourself to do whatever it took to find new ways of being in the world? Were you also prepared to leave no stones unturned until you found those ways?

Patricia Campbell arrived at a turning point when she vowed to turn her life around and do whatever it took to change her life from one she hated into a life she absolutely loved.

I first met Patricia in 2020 when she contacted me to ask if I would be willing to coach her in writing her book. This one. Upon first meeting, I was overjoyed because I could see her passion and drive for what she wished to accomplish, so we could make it fun and real all the way!

Never Ever Give Up! is a gold mine of one woman's story of how she followed through on her silent promise to herself and her children and a legacy of a road map for each woman reading about how to do the same thing for herself. A dearly held dream of a vision inspired Patricia to take steps from struggle to confidence, putting one foot in front of the other and never, ever giving up.

Through sharing tools and techniques and her captivating story of each step and choice, no matter how it unfolded, Patricia demonstrates how she became the self-made woman she knew in her heart was possible—an inspiring speaker, certified transformational life and business coach for women, and self-made millionaire.

Although details of her story will differ from yours, the underlying humanity, the yearning we all have for meaning and purpose in our lives, and finding the ways to obtain it, will give you hope and passion for taking the steps that are both right and calling to you.

Let this book be your best friend, for it will teach you how to build confidence to step forward. Let Patricia's kindness, heart, wisdom, and skills mentor you. May you always have a dream to cherish and learn how to live it out loud!

All blessings,
Junie Swadron
Psychotherapist and book-writing coach
Author of *Re-Write Your Life* and *Your Life Matters*
www.junieswadron.com

My Story

I wake up every single morning with a prayer of gratitude for my amazing life, which has been quite a journey, a hang-on-tight kind of ride. Though now I'm hanging on with open hands rather than closed fists. Every day I am filled with wonderment as I declare, "This is the best day of my life!"

I am humbled, happy, and grateful for the abundant life I have created. I broke free of the limiting patterns of failed relationships, selling out on myself, and feeling unworthy, unloved, and alone.

I live in deep gratitude for the loving, trusting relationship I now have with my husband, the cherished friendships with my children, the two amazing grandchildren who bless my life, and the friends who bring joy to me. These extraordinary relationships are a WOWZER for me!

And for over twenty years, it has been my privilege and honor to coach, mentor, and support women to create abundance in all areas of their lives. As I recount my trials and triumphs in these chapters, please pay close attention to the lessons I have learned. I share my secrets about how I transformed my biggest challenges into a life I absolutely love.

Once I discovered my passion for transformation, I applied it in many ways. Just as we can transform houses into living spaces that reflect who we are and yards into retreats with glorious flower gardens, we can also transform ourselves when we have the desire and the right tools. We can heal money issues, relationships, and low self-esteem. I can attest to these results because I have built a multi-million-dollar enterprise following my passion while creating a life I love. Compared to earlier years, my life today feels like a miracle.

Never Ever Give Up! is my way of sharing my journey and experiences with you to inspire you to know beyond a shadow of a doubt that *you,* too, can create a life you love—so much that you never want to take a holiday from it.

What does it take to overcome years of hardship, heartbreak, and feeling lost and alone, to step into a life of ease and joy, clarity, love, and belonging—a life you wholeheartedly love? The book you are holding in your hands shows you what it takes. I moved from an existence I hated to one I loved.

In these pages, I take you with me on my pilgrimage, offering insights and action steps I used to turn my breakdowns into breakthroughs. I pray that when you see what I have overcome, you will know with complete certainty that you *can* become the woman you want to be, living the life you long to live. The steps I am about to guide you through will show you the way. I believe there is a reason you are reading these words today.

I believe there is a part of you that is longing for more. More life, in all the ways that it can show up; a life of freedom that is rich, rewarding, and fulfilling.

You are not alone. Most people want more of something in their lives, like more time, money, happiness, love, vibrant health, or freedom. And often, it is what they do not want that motivates them.

That scenario described me perfectly. I knew a lot about wanting more and being dissatisfied with my life. I believe the universe speaks to us through two growth signals: our longings and our discontent.

In the workshops I offer for women ready for a life they love, I start by asking them to do a life assessment of the major areas in which we create results: Health & Well-Being, Love & Relationships, Vocation, and Time & Money Freedom. We focus on whether they feel fulfilled in those areas or if there is room for growth and change. Soon, I will ask you to examine these areas of your life to become aware of what you would love to have more, or less of, in your life.

For now, I share my story and what it took to transform my younger life, which felt like a nightmare, into what I now call my dream life. What I describe may not be easy to read; however, this story is my truth. I want you to know that I overcame these earlier circumstances and am now thriving.

I share exercises and techniques from my training, so you have practical tools to repattern any limiting beliefs, reclaim your power, and step into your greatness.

While I am not a therapist, nor do I hold any degrees in psychology, I have studied with world-renowned teachers Mary Morrissey, Lisa Nichols, and Dr. Claire Zammit to become a specialist in transformation. I am now a certified transformational life and business coach for women, a

Kundalini yoga teacher, a clinical EFT/Tapping relationship coach and practitioner, and a Re-Write Your Life Program™ facilitator. Most recently, I am honored to say I am one of only forty people (worldwide) to graduate from The Lisa Nichols Certified Transformational Trainer Program.

Initially, I studied these principles to transform my limiting beliefs. Then, the powerful changes I experienced ignited a passion in me to become certified in all of these modalities to coach and empower other women to go from stuck to unstoppable. My life is not perfect; I do, however, have the support, tools, and resilience to navigate any situations that arise. We cannot control everything that happens to us; however, rather than reacting, we have the power to decide how we respond.

There is a power in us greater than any circumstances or conditions we face. I believe we are spiritual beings on a human journey; the hero's journey, lovingly called the *shero's* journey by my wise teacher, Lisa Nichols.

As esteemed author Napoleon Hill writes, "Every failure brings with it the seed of an equivalent success." He also says, "Every adversity brings with it the seed of an equivalent advantage." As you read my story, please know that I truly believe we can transform our life no matter what our stories have been up until now. How? Never Ever Give Up!

Our history does not determine our future.

I grew up in an environment of domestic violence. I would often wake up to see my mom with another black eye, and even as a young girl, I knew her repeated story of tripping on the stairs did not ring true.

The arguing got worse as I got older. I always knew when it was time to scoot my younger sister and three brothers downstairs to play while I stayed upstairs to block the basement door and keep them out of harm's way.

My father had a brutal temper, and the arguments always led to the same scenario, with my mom running to the bathroom and trying to lock the door to escape his rage. When she did not make it in time, it always, every single time, ended with him pushing her into the dry bathtub and beating her with the wooden handle of a long back scrubbing brush while she screamed for help. I remember once when I could not bear the sounds, I pulled on his pant leg, begging him to leave her alone. He turned around with the weapon in his hand, threatening me, "Get out, or you are next!"

I lost my voice in the turbulence of those attacks. I had no one to tell and nowhere to go for safety, so I silently held it tightly clenched inside. My mom's parents and siblings lived two houses away from us, but they seemed to have no idea of what was happening, or, if they did, no one talked about it. I also tried to pretend it was not happening as I struggled to bury the shame I felt. When I started school, I never invited friends over because I did not want anyone to know what happened inside our home.

I always wondered if my mom was in denial because every night, just before my dad came home from work, she would brush her hair and put on the most beautiful shade of bright red lipstick like everything was normal. I knew how she felt in my heart and gut, but we never talked about it, and everyone acted like the beatings never happened.

I pitied my mom, but I did not want to be weak like her or be like my bully of a dad. He scared me, and I was afraid of him. So, I subconsciously believed that women were weak and that I had to guard myself against men so I would not get hurt.

My father was committed to a mental institution when I was eleven years old, in grade five. My mother then met a man, Bob, through a friend of hers, and, to this day, I still remember seeing her laugh when she was with him in a way I had never seen before. Even though there were five of us children, Bob invited us to move in with him. So, she gathered us up, and we all moved to a new town so she could start over and he could take care of us. Can you imagine—five kids under the age of eleven? He must have loved her. Many men might have said, "That was fun; now I'm out of here."

I was thrilled to leave my old life and start over. Our new situation convinced me that everything was now going to be wonderful, and we would all be happy.

I went fishing for the first time that summer. Bob took me, my sister, and brothers fishing and made sure we all caught a fish. I was young and didn't know what to call him, so I asked him, and he said he would really like it if we called him "Dad." That felt strange, although I remember thinking maybe we could be a *real* family.

I don't know why my mom did not come fishing with us, but I can imagine her at home cooking something delicious while we were out playing. She loved cooking and feeding us. Every one of her children would attest to that.

I started grade six in a small school that I had to get to on a school bus. At first, it seemed like a friendly place. I was never a shy kid and immediately made friends with the small group. Then one day, I walked into the classroom, and everyone ignored me. It was like I suddenly did not exist. It was shocking! I was devastated. What could have happened? What did I do? What did I say? I found out later that the most popular girl had spread lies about me to turn the other kids against me and make sure no one would be my friend because the boy she had a crush on was paying attention to me. I was shocked by how abruptly gossip changed my life.

The isolation left me feeling like something was wrong with me and that I was not good enough. When it turned to ridicule and outright harassment, I interpreted that to mean I was not safe to show up and shine. I judged my worth based on the actions of others and the way they treated me. I was lost and confused.

My saving grace was Lisa, the other new girl at the school, who stayed friends with me. We never talked about how they treated me; they just left her alone.

I did not have the heart to tell my mom that I didn't fit in and the other kids were bullying me. By then, she had her hands full fighting her own battles with our new dad. I had no one else to tell, so I pretended I didn't care, and that was the beginning of putting up walls to protect myself from being hurt. Even with our brand-new beginning, nothing had changed from our earlier family life.

I was alone. My bedroom became my fortress; books were my escape. Eventually, in grade eleven, I met a boy who seemed to like me. He was an older boy from out of town, unaware of my tarnished reputation from the years of schoolyard bullying.

I craved attention, and belonging to someone; he gave me more positive attention and affection than I had ever had. I pretended this boy was a charming prince. I spent hours flipping through the pages of the Sears catalog, looking at furniture and wedding rings, imagining I had someone who loved me and a home of my own where we lived happily ever after. In my imagination, I was living in a fairy tale.

Sure enough, one thing led to another, and I got pregnant. I was thrilled. I was sure I would be the best mom in the world. We were going to be the PERFECT family! At the age of sixteen, this felt like a dream come true. Unfortunately, that was an illusion, not a reality.

It was 1970, so finishing high school was out of the question, and getting married was what my mom and stepdad insisted we do. There were only two options. The first was to put the baby up for adoption, which was completely out of the question for me. Therefore, we had to get married, and in a hurry. They told me that being an unwed mother with an illegitimate child was disgraceful for my child and me.

The marriage lasted until my son was ten months old, and the guy I thought was Prince Charming turned out to be a mean SOB, just like my father and Bob. I was playing out what I knew. Freud called it the repetition compulsion. We play out the same patterns of our youth, believing we will make it all better this time.

The day I refused to let my husband bully me was when I started standing up for myself and stopped allowing circumstances to determine my future. At the time, I didn't know that's what I was doing. I learned many years later that I, and all of us, are much more powerful and have so much more potential than any situation or condition in our lives.

When that marriage ended, I had two choices for supporting myself and my baby. One was welfare, and the other was to find a job. I am not sure where the resolve came from, but something rose up in me to prove to myself that I could make it on my own, to do whatever I had to do, so I did not have to rely on anyone. I needed to believe in myself and to know who I was. I had to build my resilience muscles.

I lived in a small town, and jobs were scarce. However, I was determined to get a job and willing to apply at every business in town. Because I had worked as a waitress the entire time I was in high school, I knew how to work hard. Once I made that decision, I got a full-time job at the Royal Bank, the only bank in town, and at times I also cleaned an office for a small business. It was easy to find a loving woman to care for my son, and I am grateful for her to this day.

Life seemed good, and I felt secure looking after my son and myself. Then, my parents helped me get a small mobile home they put on a corner of their acreage. It was mine, and I was thrilled to make the payments.

My brothers would babysit for me when I did go anywhere, which was seldom, and I was happy with things just the way they were. I dated only a couple of times, but nothing of any consequence to even mention. I was busy with work and raising my fabulous and very active son. At seventeen, focusing on him and work was the level of my capacity and all I could think about, which was fine with me.

Three years later, in 1973, when I was twenty, I once again thought I could make my ideal life come true. I fell in love with the man who would become my second husband. I was young, immature in many ways, and hopeful that I could have the love and the family I desperately craved.

Did the TV shows of that era influence me, and did I use them as role models for the perfect family? Looking back, I think so. The shows *Leave it to Beaver, The Waltons,* and *The Brady Bunch* portrayed the family experience I yearned for without any idea of how it could happen for me. Was I truly conscious that this was Hollywood at its best, and none of that was real? I'm not sure, but I know I never thought about it. I just liked what I saw and the feelings I got when I saw those families. Even after my life so far, I was a young, starry-eyed girl.

I was thrilled with the birth of our daughter in October 1974. I hoped we would suddenly become a tight-knit family and I would be the love of my partner's life. That never happened. We wanted different things; we had different values. Right from the beginning, I ignored the signs, the red flags.

The relationship between us was rocky from the start, and I naively thought things would change on their own. However, we both brought our patterns to the partnership; unhealed past relationship pain, wounds, money issues, love issues, commitment issues—and unrealistic hopes.

We were young, and sometimes, you don't plan for the future when you're young. It's all about how it is right now. All I knew was that what I wanted was what I had always wanted—a family. I did not know at the time that we live our lives by design or default. We did not take the time to design anything. Instead, we jumped right into it with all of our default behaviors and unconscious beliefs. Looking back, I can see we were unskilled at love, relationship, and marriage.

There were good days, and days when I screamed from loneliness, and wanted to run away from my life of few choices. I felt trapped with a grade eleven education, limited job skills, and two young children, like being stuck in the spin cycle of a washing machine. No matter how hard I tried, I felt powerless to create the life I imagined was possible.

I felt lost, alone, and very angry. The more unstable things got, the more I tried to control everything. It felt like my emotional stability depended on that control, and it was how I coped even though I knew it was not giving me the love I so deeply desired. I had a flame burning in my heart to belong, have a partnership, and feel cherished.

There came a day in the summer of 1976 when I could no longer ignore that my marriage was not working; I feared I would never have the life I wanted. Things had deteriorated, and I remember sitting in the bankruptcy office alone with the trustee, explaining what I thought had happened. I felt like the situation had catapulted me back to my childhood—where I never, ever wanted to be again—in a place of feeling depleted on every level.

As much as I didn't want to, I had to face what happened when I was packing and moving the last boxes out of my home that the bankruptcy forfeited. The new owners stopped by with their realtor and another couple. They walked through the open front door while I was packing boxes into the van, and it was like I was invisible. I heard them going from room to room in the house that had been my dream home—the first REAL gorgeous home I'd ever had in my life. The home I thought would be the setting for the marriage I fantasized about and would house my perfect family. I could hear these people raving about the house. I listened to their words that felt like a stabbing knife ripping through me. "Wow! What a bargain. How beautiful!" I found myself shrinking and slinking out the door, so they would not see my shame and the failure I felt as they claimed this house, my house.

My upbringing was unstable, and I always felt insecure. Here I was at twenty-three with the one stable element in my life, poof, up in smoke! Just like that! It was unbearable. I hated being at this level of struggle.

I did not really know how everything had happened, but I told myself I would pay more attention now. Then, as is often the case, my life got busy, and I still kept hoping things would change. However, the truth is nothing changed because I didn't change a thing. So how could it change? Have you ever felt like you were sleepwalking through your life?

And in the blink of an eye, it was 1988. Twelve years had passed, and things had not changed for the better—they had deteriorated even more. I was still desperate for love. I was desperate to BE loved. I remember thinking that I was either unlovable or had a knack for choosing people who didn't love me—at least not the way I dreamt of being loved. I ached to be wanted, seen, and adored, to know that I mattered. Not just for sex. I could have had that. I wanted MORE.

As much as I had tried to manage things, I seemingly had no influence over my life at all, which had been out of control for as long as I could remember. I had become an overly controlling perfectionist because I thought life would become manageable, make sense, or be less complicated if *I* were in charge. However, with the combination of willful teenagers, an absent, uncommitted husband, and a dissatisfied wife, it did not go so well. I felt like a victim of my circumstances over and over, and I did not like it one bit. Life was so frustratingly hard! I was in a lifetime of broken dreams.

In this case, I sometimes feel embarrassed to say, "I did give up." I am the one who finally ended the marriage, and even after telling my story, it has taken me years to forgive myself. It isn't that I think I should have stayed. No, I knew I needed to leave, which has never changed. However, I did not have a clue how to do it or where to begin.

Divorce creates overwhelming emotions for many of us—a combination of anger, fear, resentment, and confusion. We may also feel shame or guilt. When I went through my divorce, I felt all of these emotions and more.

My marriage ended, as many do, with blame, regret, pain, and heartache. It took me years through forgiveness practices (that I now teach) to forgive us for the part we each played in the failure of our promise to each other. All of us repeat patterns until we become conscious of them.

Now I focus on the blessings that came out of that union. The gift is the family we created, and the inseparable bonds formed. My beloved son connected with the man who, I believe, was always meant to be his father, and our daughter, my best friend, was brought into this world. Together with his daughter from his first marriage, we created cherished family memories that live to this day.

Growing up, my parents told me not to complain because other people had it much worse than me. It was confusing because they may not have complained out loud, but it felt like a black cloud was always hanging over them. I also learned not to expect more out of my life and to accept the way things were, even if I did not like it. I did not want to complain; however, I truly did not want to settle for this life I was living. A part of me went along with that concept because I could not see any other way to do it. And yet, another part of me felt trapped by giving in to these conditions, creating an internal power struggle.

In 1990, I was single, twice divorced, and living with my daughter in a rented basement suite in East Vancouver, working at a so-so job, and living paycheck to paycheck. With all the changes I had made, my life was still difficult.

One night in August that year, I got into a heated argument with my sixteen-year-old daughter. In the middle of that argument, I heard my mother's voice explode out of my mouth, catapulting me back to my teenage years. Everything I always said I would never be, I became in that moment of irrepressible anger. I was shocked and shaken to the core. And I was ashamed.

I hated my life. I hated myself. I was miserable, broke, and lost. If I had taken inventory, I could have easily said I was, even after all those years, still bankrupt; financially, in my relationships, and in my self-esteem.

The one phrase I remember my mom often saying was, "I give up." In that moment, a part of me wanted to give up like she eventually did. However, the memory of witnessing her heart-breaking life fueled me into being hell-bent on never *ever* giving up.

That night, after my shocking outburst at my daughter, I made a vow to myself. I swore I would do whatever it took, however long it would take, to figure out how to create a successful life—a life that I could model for my children. I was determined in my decision. It was non-negotiable!

However, the execution of that decision was not so easy. Then, a friend told me about a workshop for women that sounded like just what I needed. "A workshop on how to make relationships work," she said. I was scared. What if it did not work? What if nothing changed *again?* In addition to the fear swelling up in me to think of spending three days at a personal growth seminar, I found out what it cost, and I froze with resistance. Are you kidding me? I was already barely able to make ends meet, so it seemed like a fortune.

Even though my friend raved about this workshop and how it had helped her, I wondered if I could just find a great self-help book and figure it out on my own. My mom taught me *do-it-yourself* to save money. Growing up, I had everything from handmade clothes to home perms. The clothes were great, and the perms worked until that time in grade eight when she permed my hair right after bleaching it. Needless to say, I developed a modest skepticism of doing it myself after a certain point.

However, money was an issue, so even if I had wanted to, I did not know how on earth I would pay for the seminar. I had no extra money and did not qualify for a credit card since I no longer had a husband or a credit rating. In those days, it was hard for a single woman to get credit without a co-signer. My husband got to keep his credit, and I had to start over.

I had every justifiable reason why the workshop was impossible. A huge part of me argued for why I couldn't do it. Surprisingly, even to me, there was also a part that felt like the workshop could be the answer to my prayers. I wasn't really a praying woman in those days, but I sure felt like a desperate woman.

Finally, I decided to let my dream win over the part of me that was afraid. I got an idea to borrow the money from a friend and, even though I had no idea how I would pay it back, I promised her that I would, no matter what! My friend loaned me the money, and I did find a way to pay it back. I was amazed that it ended up being so easy once I made the choice to follow my heart.

There is an infamous quote by William Hutchison Murray about commitment,

> Until one is committed, there is hesitancy, the chance to draw back, always ineffectiveness. Concerning all acts of initiative (and creation), there is one elementary truth, the ignorance of which kills countless ideas and splendid plans, namely: that the moment one definitely commits oneself, then Providence moves too. All sorts of things occur to help one that would never otherwise have occurred. A whole stream of events issues from the decision, raising in one's favor all manner of unforeseen incidents and meetings and material assistance, which no one could have dreamt would have come their way.

What I now know, and what I coach in my programs, is that no new process can begin and no new path can be forged, until a decision has been made. However, once you make a firm commitment, even in the absence of perfect conditions, a whole manner of activity occurs, rushing to your aid to fulfill that decision.

Those three days at that workshop were life-changing, and they opened something up inside me that had been locked and barricaded for a very long time.

I found myself in a group of other women and was, for the first time in a long time, without work or children, totally uninterrupted. During the breaks, they instructed us not to talk to anyone but to process what thoughts and feelings came up during our exercises. I never had self-reflected or looked inside myself to that degree in my life.

We did one visualization exercise, and a woman in the group started loudly sobbing. I was unaware of it for a while, but as she began wailing, I noticed I was tightly clenching my whole body. My hands squeezed into fists, I clamped my legs together and clasped my arms across my chest so tightly I could barely breathe.

Somewhere in the distance, I heard someone softly say, "It's time to let go." She said it over and over. "Let go. Let go. Let go." Somehow, that voice reached me, and I suddenly realized how much I had been holding inside me for all those years. The protective wall I had built around my heart began to crumble, and a floodgate of tears poured out of me. I could feel my heart begin to open.

Years of my parents telling me not to complain caused me to keep everything stuffed inside. I once overheard a therapist say to someone, "The tragedy isn't what happened. The tragedy is that you had no one to tell."

That was just the beginning, and it started me on a journey that I am still on today. I have invested over thirty years studying, learning, changing, and growing. As I slowly pieced it together in the years that followed, I could see the patterns and paradigms that were the fabric of my family as I was growing up.

I started to notice the limiting beliefs I carried with me that, as a mother, I was then passing on to my children. These were patterns that kept me stuck in the gap between the life I was living and the life of my dreams. I realized these beliefs caused fear, lack, aloneness, and the feeling that I was fundamentally flawed. I was determined to transform myself, so my soul could fly.

I wanted to know more about the people who seem to have it all: how they earn abundant incomes, are with the love of their life, take long family vacations, thoroughly enjoy what they do, and are truly happy from the inside out. For years, I longed to be one of those who had it all. I never finished high school and didn't know how to create a better life for myself and my family.

That argument with my daughter in 1990 ignited a blazing fire in me—I was ready to create a better life for myself, her, and for my son, who was already out on his own. I longed to be that mom I dreamt of being when I was sixteen.

I wanted financial security so I could afford a nice home for us. I also wanted to provide my children with education if they chose that, and I yearned for healthy, loving relationships. I did dream of those big life goals; I also wanted what felt like luxuries—a closet filled with clothes I loved and to give my daughter the same pleasure. I wanted a reliable car that I was proud of—a sporty red car was what I saw in my mind.

On my journey to become the woman I am today, I was willing to turn myself inside out. I was ready to rise again and again to discover myself, heal myself, and love myself. I was willing to disrupt who I was to become the woman I wanted to be. And yet, I had taken myself as far as I could on my own.

Do you find yourself relating in some way to my story? If so, please know there is a way through whatever is holding you back to own your power and make all your dreams come true—a dynamic system of transformation.

And that is where this book begins, dear reader. I want you to know that I built the life of my dreams, and you can too! Are you discontent with circumstances or conditions, ready to move into your fulfilling new life? This book can be your stepping-stone to living a life you love. Everyone has the power within themselves to change their lives for the better. You will see that with a powerful vision of what you would love, mindset mastery, and clear, actionable steps, you will experience accelerated growth and transform your results and your life into whatever you desire.

I reveal what it takes to go from feeling powerless to being powerful. I share the lessons I learned and the habits, limiting patterns, and beliefs I overcame to start living a life that I positively love. I am an ordinary woman who has made some extraordinary decisions. I have made it my life's mission to understand how to bridge the gap between the life I wanted and the one I was living.

The good news is—because I invested over thirty years learning proven, repeatable, reliable systems of how to create results that gave me the life I love, you don't have to spend thirty years getting there.

During those years, I was like a thirsty sponge, soaking up every ounce of knowledge I could find from books, courses, and teachers around the world who shared their wisdom. I once traveled to India, where I lived for six months studying the ancient philosophy of yoga and Ayurveda. This is what I discovered: as the famous yoga teacher B.K.S. Iyengar says, "You do not need to seek freedom in some distant land, for it exists within your own body, heart, mind, and soul. Illuminated emancipation, freedom, unalloyed and untainted bliss await you, but you must choose to embark on the Inward Journey to discover it."

In Iyengar's book *Light on Life,* I first learned we all have limiting patterns that hold us back, keep us stuck, and block us from our true selves. However, once we become aware of them, we can transform the underlying beliefs that keep them in place and break free.

My determined pursuit brought me to Mary Morrissey, Brave Thinking Institute™, and to the DreamBuilder™ system of transformation, a unique approach to personal and spiritual development that sets this program apart from others.

My quest then led me to the Queen of empowered speaking, Lisa Nichols, Founder of Motivating the Masses, where I rediscovered my voice and learned a dynamic new way to tell my story.

From there, I was blessed to find Feminine Power™, with Dr. Claire Zammit. I am honored to be in an exclusive Mastermind group with her.

Through powerful teachings in the many programs that I participated in, I developed an innate understanding of how transformation happens at a cellular level. Taking what I learned from theory to application, I applied these proven systems to my life to transform limiting beliefs. As a result, my company, Crystallize Coaching, emerged. I am living my soul's purpose as a transformational life and business coach, mentoring and supporting women to create change.

I believe with all my heart that when you show up fully and make a decision for yourself, you too will discover how to tap into your power to become the woman you dream of being, living the life you dream of living.

Master Your Results

If something stands between you and the results you want in your life, I am here to share some powerful tools to help you achieve the results you desire. My intention is that, when you finish reading this book, you have the power to create your destiny with greater clarity on your dreams—and you feel confident in the ability that lives in you to achieve those goals and dreams.

Our dreams are often born out of the challenges we face or the pain we experience. We live in a Universe that speaks to us through two growth signals: our longing and our discontent. We feel longing when we desire something we have yet to create. And we feel discontent when we do not want our current circumstances. Both feelings—longing and discontent—are catalysts for growth within us.

Whether it is the pain of a problem or a profound yearning for something else, these two energies are essential for creating new results in our lives.

Reverend Dr. Michael Beckwith has a great quote in which he says that to change our life, "We are often pushed by pain until we are pulled by a vision."

I have shared my stories of living with frustration and discontent year after year and how the burning desire for the life I wanted finally forced me to make a change.

In this chapter, I share principles to help you transform your longing and discontent into new results. The principles I share come from the DreamBuilder Program, wherein I am certified and thrilled to teach. It's a proven, reliable, repeatable system for helping you create what matters most to you. Over the past forty years, Mary Morrissey developed this system of success, and tens of thousands of people worldwide have used it to create lives they love living.

I am grateful to be able to give you key principles you can apply right now to help you create a fulfilling life. These principles are what I teach in all my workshops and coaching programs about how to master your results.

Every one of us is creating results in our lives all day, every day. The question is, are we happy with those results? Some you may love, and others, maybe not. Perhaps, as I did, you have conditions or situations right now in some area of your life that are causing you pain. It could be in your career, the amount of money you have, or in a relationship, perhaps with your health, or the lack of free time.

I have good news for you; no matter the situation, how long you have been living it, or how big of a challenge it seems, you have the power to create the exact results you would love to have in your life.

You have the power within yourself to change your life for the better. This power is available to everyone, no matter their circumstances, situation, or condition. You have already tapped into this power, possibly without even realizing it.

Think about the last time you had something important to do with very little time, yet somehow you found a way to get it done. Perhaps you negotiated for more time or delegated tasks to accomplish everything. Or maybe you just manifested a massive burst of productivity and got it done.

Are you thinking, "It's easy enough to say that, but if I have all that power, then why haven't I been able to use it until now?"

The answer is that this power has always existed, but not everyone knows how to harness it. Your ability to access this power is not automatic. You must consciously learn how to harness and work with this power that operates by the invisible laws of success. The possibilities are endless when you know how to work with these laws.

These invisible laws are comparable to electricity, which enables us to create amazing things. Electricity has ALWAYS existed. No human invented this invisible force; Benjamin Franklin learned how to work with it.

Achieving your dream life is like plugging into an electrical socket for power. You cannot make electricity work as you want it to; you must work within its invisible properties.

Just like electricity, the invisible laws of success work the same way, every time, no matter who you are, regardless of your gender, location, or history. Once you align with the Laws of the Universe, you can shine brightly no matter where you are or how little success you've had in the past.

Are you as surprised as I was to learn that many people live their lives by default? By default, I mean going with the flow, taking it as it comes, just coping. I lived that way until I learned that highly successful people create a life *by design*. In other words, they set a clear intention for what they would love and consciously create what they want in their life.

That night in the summer of 1990, when I heard my mother's voice in my heated words to my daughter, was a time in my life when longing and discontent forced me to change. I pray you do not wait until you get a wake-up call, as I did. Had I listened to the first whispers of the Universe trying to get my attention, I would have begun this journey eons earlier and may have started living a life I love much sooner. Although I was only thirty-seven, in many ways, I felt old beyond my years, like I had already lived a lifetime.

My mentor, Mary Morrissey, says, "Some people live 90 years, and some people live the same year 90 times." That was me. I had been living the same year over and over, feeling frustrated with my lack of progress and results.

Today, I love knowing how and why results happen or do not happen, regardless of how much effort I exert.

When I learned what is called "The Results Formula" in my certification training, a light bulb went off, and it was the beginning of me going from victim to co-creator with Life.

I felt like a victim for most of my life. I thought life was happening TO me until I learned I could change my beliefs and patterns.

Once I got that—*really got it*—I sensed that I had the power to create whatever I truly wanted. I began to notice when I felt powerless and, conversely, like the co-creator of my destiny. I was seeing things differently, and I had a new awareness that sparked my soul. I then began asking new questions about life.

Knowing the language of success helps you create new results, possibilities, and outcomes. This language produces the results you want. And once you consciously understand this language, you can apply it to any area of your life that you want to improve.

Although I have always known that action is a significant ingredient in creating results, I learned that what precedes action are a few key steps. During my training at Brave Thinking Institute, I studied this effective method of mastering results.

I wish I had been aware of the connection between thoughts and results earlier when I believed that effort and hard work were what it took to succeed. I am happy to tell you there is an easier way to create the results and the life you desire.

The Results Formula

There are four major areas in which we experience our results: Health & Well-Being, Love & Relationships, Vocation, and Time & Money Freedom. And every one of us achieves results in each area of life.

The results you are getting in your life in these areas perfectly reflect your awareness. A pattern creates your results, or what I call The Results Formula.

The formula begins like this: your thoughts cause your feelings. When you think positive thoughts, you feel happy. You feel anxious when you think scary thoughts, and sometimes your heart beats faster. You might feel stressed or overwhelmed when you think of everything on your to-do list and how there's not enough time to do it all. When you think about a success you have achieved, you feel more confident and uplifted. Your thoughts affect your physiology.

You express your feelings through your actions. Here is an experiment you can try. Imagine the physical posture and facial expression of someone unhappy. In my workshops, I find that everyone always knows how to do this. Shoulders slumped, head down, face sullen. Take a moment and model that yourself. How does that feel?

Now, shake it off. Put your hands in front of you or in the air and shake it off. And now assume the body position of someone confident, happy, or who had major success and feels unstoppable! Stand up, pull your shoulders back and lift your arms high. Walk around the room like this with a huge smile. How do you feel? Do you sense the difference between this posture and how you felt when acting unhappy?

Our feelings lead to our actions or reactions and sometimes to no action. When we feel confident and energized, we take different actions than when we feel depressed, frustrated, or sad. Actions, and not taking action (i.e., inertia), cause results in our lives. Joan Baez says, "Action is the antidote to despair."

Your thoughts cause your feelings, your feelings cause your actions, and your actions cause your results.

This is the Law of Cause and Effect, yet many people do not know this law. They only look at their results—circumstances and conditions in their lives—and call those "be-causes." For example, I can't start a new career be-cause I'm too old or be-cause I don't know enough, or I would lose all of my benefits. I can't take time off be-cause I don't have the money or be-cause I don't have the vacation time, and my boss won't let me. I can't find the love of my life be-cause I'm not young enough, thin enough, or attractive enough. I can't, I can't, I can't be-cause, because, be-CAUSE!

The true cause of our results is in our minds, in our thoughts. Our results are caused by what we think—the first cause.

If you want to know what you've been thinking, look at your results. Your results never lie. If you want to create new results in your life, the first place to look is at what you have been thinking.

None of us gets a break from thinking. We are doing it all the time. Studies show that we have thousands of thoughts every day. And one of the most life-changing things I have ever learned is that we can choose our thoughts. We can let our old habitual thoughts run our lives or decide to change them. Monitoring our thoughts and self-talk is essential to create expanded, positive results. We cannot think negatively and expect to produce positive outcomes.

We all have well-worn thoughts that become habitual and form a pattern. When I began to understand this factor, it was a turning point for me and the emergence of a new mastery in my life. This knowledge deciphered the code to create the results I dreamed were possible.

Key #1

Pay Attention to Your Thoughts

When we want to create different results in our life, the first key is to pay attention to what we are thinking. Another way to say this is, "Notice what you're noticing."

Take a moment and close your eyes. Then notice your feet and pay attention to whether you are wearing socks or shoes, or if your feet are bare and touching the ground. Notice that you feel your body sitting in your seat and be aware if your shoulders are tense or relaxed. Notice that you can feel yourself breathing. Now, notice your ability to notice these elements of your body.

You can do the same thing with your thoughts. Notice what you are thinking, and also observe how your thoughts affect how you are feeling. Sometimes, we do not know what we are thinking until we notice a particular feeling, like stress, fear, or maybe excitement.

When that happens, pause, and ask yourself what you were just thinking.

Developing the ability to notice what exact thoughts may have caused your feelings is essential. When we know what we have been thinking and learn the skill of choosing our thoughts, ensuring we align them with the results we are aiming for, we can manifest the outcomes we desire.

Let's apply this concept of The Results Formula and start noticing what you are thinking about yourself and your life.

If you and I were working together on planning your future, one of the first things I would ask you is to assess your level of fulfillment and satisfaction in the quadrants of your life that I mentioned earlier. Then we would look at your current results to see if there is anything you would like to be different and more fulfilling.

Have you ever *really* examined your life? Do you know what is required to live a life you love?

To help you, here is an assessment questionnaire for you to look at in each key area: Health & Well-Being, Love & Relationships, Vocation, and Time & Money Freedom.

Let's start with your dreams. You may not know your dream; however, you sense or know there is something "more" possible.

Maybe you are nervous that if you focus on only one dream, you will let other dreams and ideas go unrealized. You may know your dream as I did, and you are a woman passionate about it—but you are not yet creating the ideal results.

It is possible, like other women, that you think you have tried everything, and nothing seems to be working. Or you might be ready to revisit an earlier dream and manifest it now because you know this is your time.

Are you a woman who has achieved great success and you are afraid that, if you reach for a higher level, you'll lose any success you have already achieved? Or perhaps you have achieved a high level of success, and yet, you are not feeling totally fulfilled or making the difference you want to make?

I believe every one of us has a dream inside, even if we still strive to find or achieve it. The awareness exercise we are about to do helps connect you with your dream and will propel you on the path toward the results you would love. I offer this exercise at every Vision Workshop I facilitate.

Life Assessment Exercise

Get your journal and use a new page for each of the four domains I talked about: Health & Well-Being, Love & Relationships, Vocation, and Time & Money Freedom.

Take some time here and, on each page, journal your thoughts and feelings about how fulfilled you are with your results. Sometimes we know we are not happy or fulfilled in a particular area, and we are longing for something different.

Sometimes we have settled for the way it is because we think there is no option, or we feel stuck in our ability to change our results. There are times we tolerate situations or conditions in our health, relationships, money, business, or work.

We have tried to make changes, but we can't, or they last for a little while until it returns to how it was. At that point, we feel stuck or frustrated, sometimes giving up. Thomas Edison said, "Our greatest weakness lies in giving up. The most certain way to succeed is always to try just one more time." As you do this assessment, this may be that one more time.

On a scale of one to five for each area, how fulfilled are you with your current results? One means you are not fulfilled at all and five is completely fulfilled. Make a note of that number in your journal.

Now, take a moment and reflect on your Life Assessment. As you looked at your current results, you rated yourself on a scale of one to five for each area. Pay attention to your thoughts around those results. No self-judgment, please. Your responses are not good or bad or right or wrong. They are what they are at this point in your life. Like when using a GPS, to get where we want to end up, we need to know where we are NOW.

As you look at your numbers, see if you notice any longing or discontent. Would you like anything to be different than what you are seeing? When you are unaware of something, you cannot change it.

Look at the rating in each area and circle the areas with the lowest rating. Now let me ask you, how long have you felt this way? How long has this area of your life been trying to get your attention? Answering this is important; do not rush it. Take your time and write down whatever comes up for you.

What is having an ongoing lack of fulfillment costing you, not living the life you desire, or doing what you know you long to do with your gifts and talents? What is your soul whispering that is yet unlived and, so far, not done? Remember, we never get yesterday back.

We devote focused time to this process in my workshops. It is easier in a group setting because it helps to know others are having unwanted results or are feeling stuck in a recurring situation. Although this book does not provide you with a group setting like my workshops, just know that you are not alone and other women with similar challenges are possibly reading these same pages, having similar thoughts and feelings as you are. Everything I have discovered in my education as a coach and in my work with my clients tells me that there are common predominant issues women face.

I remember the first time I heard a woman share something that was a similar issue to one I had. I was shocked and, at the same time, relieved. Until then, I thought I was the only one who had that issue and felt shameful about it. That experience alone was a catalyst for me to stay in group coaching, where it was safe to speak my truth. It is why I continue to offer group programs and women's circles.

I was unaware that I kept trying to create my dream life on top of shame, regret, and blame. I dimmed my light because I was stuck in my childhood story of not being good enough. I hid out in many ways for fear of judgment until I realized that my judgments about myself were the harshest. Sometimes we do not even know we are still living in chapters one to three of our life story and that we have the power to write and live the rest of the chapters.

Many women are embarrassed to realize they have been clinging to old stories that stop them from reaching for the stars because they fear failure. Sometimes that seems the safer option, but the cost is far greater in the end. So, take your time to reflect on the payoff for you holding on to unreleased shame, playing small, and replaying demeaning stories—stifling creativity keeps us stuck and often unhappy.

You have the power from this moment forward to create the results you set your heart on, whatever your results have been up until now. It all starts with noticing your thoughts, then knowing how to master them. Either we consciously choose our thoughts to create our desired results, or we keep unconsciously thinking the same thoughts, getting the same repetitive results. As Henry Ford said, "If you always do what you've always done, you'll always get what you've always got." Knowing the language of success will help you overcome any difficulty you face.

It is important to honor your discontent and not make it wrong or feel bad about it. Something magnificent is happening with you right now; it is this thing called Life! Life constantly seeks a greater, fuller, more expanded expression of itself. Look at nature and how it is continually growing and expanding. For example, the famous Angel Oak tree in South Carolina is sixty-five feet high. Its longest branch reaches out one hundred and eighty-seven feet, and some branches even drill back into the ground and begin to grow back upward.

One way you can recognize this pull to something *more* is by the discontent you feel in any area of your life. Once you know how to recognize and then honor dissatisfaction, you begin to discover the answers to the mysteries of life.

This degree of recognition is your starting point to get crystal clear about what you would love. This step puts a spoke in the wheel of ongoing default patterns and then designing your ideal life. Think of it like disrupting a repetitive cycle of your least favorite song.

Once you know that you can choose whether to create your life by design or by default, you can bring about everything you are yearning for in this world. The preface to expressing your dream life is to notice and honor the discontent you feel in any area of your life.

If you are feeling unhappy, disappointed, contracted, or not shining your light in the world, try imagining the expansion of your life. By now, you have likely figured out that what you long for is most often the antidote to your discontent.

Highly successful people begin with the end result in mind. They become clear on what they want, and they envision the outcome. Because where your attention goes, energy flows.

Key #2
Design Your Dream Life

Designing your dream life is the second key to creating a life you love. You must plan for the results you want to produce. Having a clearly defined blueprint is equally as vital to the success of building your dream as it is to building a house.

Achieving a higher level of success and birthing your dream life requires conscious planning. In *Think and Grow Rich,* one of the books I refer to often in my coaching programs, Napoleon Hill says, "Success comes to those who become success conscious."

Many people live their entire lives without this kind of intentional forethought. For example, research shows that they spend more time organizing a weekend vacation than planning their lives.

When you become clear on what you want in life, you begin to see opportunities, circumstances, and resources that you would have otherwise missed. It is time to imagine what is possible for you.

Whether it is owning a business, doing what you love, having financial freedom, living in your dream home in the mountains, or falling in love with your soulmate, holding a vision of your dream life is exhilarating!

Your destiny to live a powerful life fills your heart and calls to you in the quiet moments; in those moments, you feel ALIVE! You feel free, ecstatically enjoying each day, living in alignment with your brilliance and shining your light.

What would you love to be, do, have, and create? Designing your dream is a critical key to mastering your results. It is the secret sauce to successfully building your dreams and creating a new reality.

What do you want? What would you love for your life? Here is an exercise to help you gain clarity on your dream, in all areas of your life. **Clarity is power!**

We do this exercise at every workshop I lead, whether the focus is building your business, creating more wealth, finding love, or overcoming the fear of showing up and speaking out.

Visioning Exercise

First, bring to mind the four areas of your life that we looked at earlier: Health & Well-Being, Love & Relationships, Vocation, and Time & Money Freedom.

- Health & Well-Being – Call forth an image of your health and well-being. How would you love to feel in your body? What activities would you engage in? How is your energy? In this picture, you are looking and feeling amazing! What would you love?

- Love & Relationships – Do you yearn for a deep, loving relationship? Do you long to deepen or have more harmony in an existing relationship? How is that relationship in your vision? Is there discontent or discord that requires resolving? What would you love? Have you met, or would you love to meet your soulmate? Are you surrounded by supportive people who love, encourage, and celebrate you?

- Vocation – What kind of work would you love to do? How do you see yourself expressing your natural gifts and talents? Who else is in the picture with you? Do you have your own business? Are you a successful entrepreneur? Do you have colleagues or an employer who supports your success? What would you love?

- Time & Money Freedom – What would you love for the flow of money in your life? How much financial wealth would you love? Do you have financial freedom? What would you do with that money? Go on a trip? Live in the home you have always wanted? Where is your home located? How have you decorated it? Would you love to give to a cause that has deep meaning for you? What would you do with your time? Would you relax and play more or spend more time with your family?

I have successfully used and taught the following method to many women over the years to ensure their success.

Now that you have thoroughly considered what you would love in these four quadrants of your life, it is your turn!

Start with a grounding practice. Go somewhere quiet where you will be uninterrupted for about thirty minutes. With eyes open or closed, take a few long, deep, slow breaths and relax into your body. If you notice any tension in your body, breathe into those places.

You have the power and authority to create and live your life any way you choose. You are empowered to write the rest of the pages in the book of your life *by design.*

This is your time! Gazing from high above you, look down upon the landscape of your current life.

What if you believed in yourself and trusted that the entire universe was organizing itself around your success and you couldn't fail? What would you be doing? Who is with you? How does it feel? Breathe deeply and bring in sounds, colors, and textures. Tune into your heart and your higher self and let them lead the way. Free your imagination. Dream BIG!

The key to visualizing your ideal life is to see pictures of it that are so real that you form an emotional bond with what you envision. So be descriptive. What would you *feel and see* as you wake up in your dream home, spend a perfect day in your dream vocation, enjoy time with the people who matter most to you, and have the ease of financial freedom? Passionately feeling it is the salient ingredient.

Using all of your senses to anchor these desires internally is essential to growing into the woman you see yourself becoming. See it, feel it, know it, get excited, claim it. LOVE IT! Let your imagination go like you did when you were a kid. Envision your life in detail as though it is all happening right now. Our subconscious mind only responds to NOW and does not know the difference between fantasy and reality, so allow yourself to imagine a life that makes you feel ALIVE!

Imagine that it is three years from now, and everything you wanted has completely worked out. You have all the resources required for your dream life to manifest. What would you LOVE?

Why three years into the future? Because our subconscious doesn't know what is possible in three years. If we think of one year from now, our mind might object that our dream cannot happen that soon and argue with thoughts like, "You didn't do that last year. What makes you think you will do it this year?" However, three years is far enough into the future to suspend any disbelief that surfaces.

Put aside any urge to figure out HOW this result is going to happen. This exercise is your magic wand for your inner vision and sensing the dream version of your life.

The final step is to write about your beautiful vision in the first person, present tense, as though it is happening right now. Open a fresh page in your journal, get some beautiful paper, or make a living document on your computer. At the top, write, *"I am so happy and grateful now that..."* And at the bottom, write, *"This or something even better."*

Only write what you *want*, not what you do *not* want, and state it in the positive. In other words, instead of writing, "I am now out of debt," write, "I live in financial abundance," or "I am financially free." When you write as though everything is happening right now, your subconscious believes it is true! That is why it is so essential to know what you would love, write it out, and claim it NOW.

After you write your dream life as you see and feel it, the next vital step is to read this vision *every single day*. You can add details to the description as you imagine more of your beautiful life unfolding. This vision is the blueprint for your dream life.

Let me tell you why that first step of knowing what you want is so important. We create everything twice. First, in thought, then in form. Think about this book, the pen you are taking notes with, and the paper you are writing on. Someone had an idea, and then it became an invention. If you think about it, every tangible thing in your life was a thought before it became a reality. Someone had to think it up before they could create it. And that is what you are doing today with your future life. You are designing your vision, designing your dreams, designing your life! There is often at least one *"How?"* question that I hear from my coaching clients. They ask me, "How do I know this is the right dream for me? How can I know this is what I'm supposed to be doing?"

If you also have these questions, I will tell you that you are worthy of any dream in your heart. The real question is, "Is the dream worthy of you?"

You will dedicate your precious time and energy to something in this lifetime, so you want to be sure it is worthy of you—the way to determine that before deciding on your dream is to *test* it.

Here are five questions to evaluate your dream to see if the vision you wrote for yourself is worthy of you.

1. Does it give me life?
2. Does it align with my core values?
3. Does it cause me to grow?
4. Does it require help from a higher power?
5. Does it have good in it for others?

You want a YES to all five questions before you decide to move forward with any action steps toward your vision.

If there is a NO somewhere in there, it's okay. That means you have an opportunity to lean into that dream a little more. Doing this exercise will give you certainty and confidence to commit to your vision with all your heart. And when you do that, without knowing *how* it will all come together, you experience new results in your life.

**"The most valuable way
you can contribute to the world
is to become your greatest self
in your lifetime."
—Patricia Campbell**

Key #3
Courageously Decide

The vision you have designed now calls for courage. Making a firm decision to stay committed to what you sense is possible for you is the key to bringing your dream into reality—even in the absence of knowing HOW.

Our decisions influence our results and significantly impact our lives. To create what matters most, it is important to make empowered decisions. Successful people make firm decisions without procrastinating.

The late Bob Proctor, renowned life coach and best-selling author, said,

> There is a single mental move you can make which, in a millisecond, will solve enormous problems for you. It has the potential to improve almost any personal or business situation you will ever encounter, and it could literally propel you down the path to incredible success. We have a name for this magic mental activity. It is called... DECISION.

The power behind my becoming a millionaire and creating financial freedom came from having a crystal-clear vision, a burning desire, and making a firm decision.

The turning point for me was that night in 1990 after my shameful outburst at my daughter. With every cell of my being, I decided that no matter what, I would become the mother and woman I had always dreamt of being in my heart and soul. This decision came from a place deep inside me that was relentless. I am not saying I mastered it instantly. The truth is, I did not. If it were that easy, we would wave a magic wand for the life we wished for to suddenly appear.

The shero's journey includes trials and tribulations for all of us. Whatever your circumstances, please know they offer the challenge and opportunity to become your most fabulous self. I called my painful circumstances "my dark night."

The phrase, *dark night of the soul,* is often used to describe an extremely difficult or painful period in one's life. Yet, it is also a time of profound transition, when something greater seeks to emerge in us through the difficulties we experience. Every person on the planet has, is, or will experience a dark night; it is paramount for our evolution.

In his book *Care of The Soul*, Thomas Moore writes about soul power and how we can tap into it. He says, "It comes first of all from living close to the heart, and not at odds with it. Therefore, paradoxically, soul power may emerge from failure, depression, and loss."

**"Dark nights invite you to
find your inner light."
—Patricia Campbell**

In the program Standing Firm When Your World Is Shaking, I coach women experiencing a challenging situation to find a way to relate to it that is empowering. I assure them it is okay to have a dark night, but it is essential not to let it overtake us. Until I studied these principles, I was making the chapters of my life become my whole story. It can be otherwise.

We truly can rewrite and heal the stories of our lives. The Dalai Lama is quoted as saying, "One must learn to take a long view." In other words, learn to hold our present difficulty in the context of a much bigger story.

Before I learned to look for the gifts buried in my life experiences, I often felt sorry for myself and got stuck in frustration. Now, with any challenge, big or small, I ask myself, "Is there something to learn or any possible opportunities to be found in this experience?"

Lisa Nichols refers to these challenges as gifts wrapped in sandpaper, which creates some levity for me.

It took an unyielding commitment for me to move beyond my story of misery. Once I did, though, I realized I was not alone in my pain. We are all on this incredible hero-and-shero's journey, the catalyst for growing in wisdom, expanding our capacity, and more connection to the infinite within us.

We can allow our problems to make us bitter and angry, and become the victims of the conditions. Or we can face them and use them as the impetus for a transformation.

Jean Shinoda Bolen, M.D., a psychiatrist, Jungian analyst, an internationally known author and speaker, and women's advocate, says, "Nobody gets through life without a degree of suffering or betrayal or illness or loss. The question is, every time that dark quality comes into our lives, what do we do? How do we respond? What have we learned? How can we grow through this?"

I would not wish what I have experienced on anyone. However, I do wish for everyone the blessing of growth and wisdom I gained from those experiences.

I kept moving forward and began transforming my struggle and poverty mindset after my heart-opening experience in that first workshop in 1990 and the following personal growth programs I attended. The instructions were always to write the results I wanted to create in my life, and one of the first desires I had was to have millionaire consciousness.

I honestly wasn't sure what that meant or how on earth it could happen. I think I heard other women talking about it, and I knew people who were what I considered to be wealthy. What I really wanted was to embody the life I saw them live. I longed for my daughter and me to be out of the basement suite in East Vancouver and have a car I was not afraid would break down every time I drove it. I wanted freedom. I wrote down that I was ready for millionaire consciousness.

Even though I did not connect the dots at the time, I started paying more attention to possibilities. While I did not yet have a formula for the new life I wanted to create, I did start to embrace a new way of thinking. And I had an open heart for the first time in forever.

I had no idea at the time how powerful an open heart can be. I know now, and I teach women, that an open heart generates a greater flow of abundance in *all* the ways abundance exists.

Let's look at how it all unfolded for me so you can see what is possible for you. First was the fun part, envisioning an abundant life—a life I would love. Then, once I let go of my past and began healing my heart, I thought about what I would love. I wanted millionaire consciousness. And I wanted to meet and marry my forever man.

I began to expand my thinking by reading things like the quote by Henry David Thoreau:

> If one advances confidently in the direction of his dreams, and endeavors to live the life which he has imagined, he will meet with a success unexpected in common hours. He will put some things behind, will pass an invisible boundary; new, universal, and more liberal laws will begin to establish themselves around and within him; or the old laws be expanded, and interpreted in his favor in a more liberal sense, and he will live with the license of a higher order of beings.

When Thoreau says, "If one advances confidently in the direction of his dreams," I understand this to mean that we must confidently decide to go for our dream and courageously take action.

I immersed myself in learning everything I could about how to keep my heart open and increase my awareness of how to create success. I was highly motivated to change from the woman I was into the woman I longed to be and to change my life into the life I yearned to live. I read books, went to every personal growth event I could find, and began volunteering as an assistant with the organization that held the first workshop I attended.

I did what, for me, was the unthinkable and began sharing my feelings with a select few women I discovered I could trust. It took a safe, sacred space with shared agreements for me to open up. Creating a sacred and safe space is now a significant component of all my programs and workshops with women.

We cannot feel free to open up and look at ourselves and our situation unless it is safe to do so. We create safety when we mutually agree on no repercussions for what we share and no judgment toward ourselves and others. Without that, we hesitate to open up and share our vulnerabilities because it feels too personal or shameful. So, we try to protect ourselves by holding it all inside and not looking at it.

Once I started looking at myself and my life, I recognized how some patterns served me and others did not. My awareness expanded as I began shedding my protection, like peeling the layers of an onion.

I also identified and stopped some critical self-talk, like clinging to my old beliefs that I was not good enough and I was better off pushing people away. I stopped focusing on changing my outer circumstances and focused on transforming my inner self. The most significant change I made was to stop dating the wrong men.

We will talk more about your unconscious patterns in Key #7, where I give you an exercise to help you uncover some of those patterns so you can begin to identify anything that might be in the way of creating results you would love.

At the age of thirty-seven, I committed to change. The cost of feeling like a failure as a mother was the motivation I needed to do whatever I had to do. I had never been that committed to myself in my life. Lo and behold, I discovered that the observation by W.H. Murray that I shared earlier was accurate. "All sorts of things occur to help one that would never otherwise have occurred. A whole stream of events issue from the decision, raising in one's favor all manner of unforeseen incidents and meetings and material assistance, which no one could have dreamt would have come their way." Once I committed to staying in action and doing the work, a whole stream of events did start to unfold.

I tell my clients that acquiring the habit of making definite, unwavering decisions requires courage and is a key factor that supports us in accelerating our dreams. Being decisive is the hallmark of all successful people, a trait Napoleon Hill discovered as a commonality amongst the most successful people he studied.

An unfolding happens, even if we do not see it at the time. My life was shifting in response to that deep commitment to myself, though I was unaware of that connection while the changes were happening.

I am aware now and felt called to understand how transformation occurs. So, I take my experiences and connect the dots for both me and you.

Now that you have learned about the power of decision, let's move forward and reveal what we add to the recipe to guarantee success.

Key #4
Burning Desire

Once you create a clear picture and decide to commit, the next key is to use your feelings to build a burning desire to support that image. People who flourish put their passion into their vision of success. In the book, *Secret of the Ages,* Robert Collier writes, "What one thing do you desire above everything else in life? Whatever it is, you can have it."

Whatever you wholeheartedly desire, with singleness of purpose, is within your reach. Wallace Wattles says in the book *A Road to Prosperity*, "The first and all-important essential is to know what this one thing is. Before you can win your heart's desire, you must get clearly fixed in your mind's eye what it is that you want."

I believe your heart yearns for something more, which is why you are reading this book. Is there a conviction within you that keeps calling, like a soul song, that you can be, do, or have whatever you desire? That impulse within you is the infinite side of you, your higher self. The most powerful creators I know, and have had the pleasure of learning from, are women who co-create with a higher power.

For many years I wondered, "What is my purpose?" The answers I received had me examine my core values and listen very closely to what I would love and made me feel more *aliveness*. I spent time in quietness, learning to listen to what my soul was saying. I began to notice where I felt aligned with the truth of who I am in my heart and what I wanted to give and create. Knowing who I am, the difference I desire to make, and who I am here to serve is still my guiding light.

Discovering and living from your purpose connects you to the deeper truth of who you are and the fulfillment of your destiny. Like a caterpillar becoming a butterfly, changing from one form to another requires a radical transformation. During the cocoon transition, the wings are strengthened enough to carry it through the next phase of the creature's life. That tells me their struggle and commitment to undergoing change are imperative for their metamorphosis.

The events of my transition included losing my job, which at the time left me feeling crushed and lost for a while. Although I did not love that job, it provided the only security I had. It was a shock, and I remember thinking how unfair it was when I had been so committed to creating a better life. It seemed that some outside circumstance or influence kept dictating who and what I could be, do, and have in my life. I felt like there was someone or something *outside* of me that always controlled my destiny. I was a victim to whichever way the wind was blowing.

I felt powerless. But I had a daughter to take care of and quitting on her was not an option for me, so self-pity had to take a back seat to finding a new job. Without that incentive, I may have succumbed to the defeat I often felt.

Having a purpose that is bigger than ourselves is one of the greatest motivators I know. I had made a promise to my son and daughter to be the best mother I could be, which mattered deeply to me. It was reason enough to push me past my thoughts of giving up. In a way, it was for my self-respect.

Do you know what your "why" is? What motivates you to push past your limits and keep going even when you do not feel like it? That reason *why* can be what gets us out of bed in the morning. It can also be what causes us to dig deep and find a way to create the results we desire, even when we think we have exhausted all possibilities.

What is it that unleashes your power and makes quitting not an option? If you are not yet crystal clear, beyond a shadow of a doubt, what that burning desire is, I invite you to put this book down and spend some quiet time in contemplation to find that answer. Do it now; do not wait one more minute because the chances of you doing it later, even if you think you will, are not good. There is a paradigm, or common pattern of delay and distraction that causes us to forget even when our intentions are noble.

Using the power of purpose to tap into your reserves of energy, courage, and resolve when facing a challenge is the determining factor for victory. Knowing your *why* is essential to achieving the vision of your life that excites you.

In *Think and Grow Rich*, Hill talks about desire being the starting point of all achievement. He says, "Wishing will not bring riches. But desiring riches with a state of mind that becomes an obsession, then planning definite ways and means to acquire riches, and backing those plans, with persistence which does not recognize failure, will bring riches." Hill also says, **"Practical dreamers DO NOT QUIT."**

Thomas Edison dreamed of a lamp that could be operated by electricity. Despite more than ten thousand failures, he stood by that dream until it became a reality.

Maybe you, like Edison with his all-consuming obsession, know what yours is. If you do not, or perhaps have given up what you did know somewhere along the way, become determined to (re)discover it. If that feels hard and you need some help uncovering your greatest longings and biggest discontents, contact me or reach out to someone you trust to assist you.

Study every person you can think of who has achieved lasting success, and you will find that they all share a deep desire and a definite purpose as their starting point. Napoleon Hill is one of the clearest examples of someone whose work and words have motivated me. Another was learning about Charles Dickens, who experienced the tragedy of unrequited first love. It is said this challenge penetrated the depths of his soul, transforming him into one of the world's greatest authors and inspiring him to write David Copperfield, among many other extraordinary books.

When I lost my job, my burning desire in life was to be happy and to be my definition of a good mother, which meant taking care of our basic needs first and foremost. One of the greatest gifts I received from my mother was her standard of family necessities. No matter what, there was always a warm, decent home, an abundance of food in the house, and no shortage of clean clothes. When I became a mother myself, I considered those non-negotiable necessities.

With that resolve, I reached out to everyone I knew after I lost my job, and it was not long before I was offered a new position with a considerable increase in income. The first thing I did was upgrade my car to a beautiful red, reliable one that made me feel like a queen.

After I had been in the new job long enough to save money and feel secure, I felt confident enough to move us out of that basement suite and into a beautiful, two-level townhouse. The rent and car payments required the biggest portion of my paycheck. But, driving that vehicle and living in a nice neighborhood in a classy new place with my daughter was worth every dime.

As I studied throughout the years, I realized that we all have unconscious patterns and limiting beliefs that dictate how much abundance we can allow ourselves in the first place and how much abundance, love, wealth, and happiness we can sustain. Until this astonishing discovery, I kept playing out my beliefs centered around my feelings of not being good enough. I remember often thinking, in that new job, that I did not know what I was doing. I was sure I was not doing as good a job as the woman who had previously held the position.

Sure enough, a year later, I was laid off, leading me back down the spiral of some very negative feelings that fueled my low self-esteem. If I were to coach my younger self today, I would tell her that to maintain abundance in any form, we must commit to standing guard against those self-critical thoughts.

The words you have been saying to yourself forever are the ones your subconscious collects and stores, and they hold power because we accept them. So, whether intentional or not, when we are habitually critical of ourselves, those comments run the show. Do not do that to yourself. Words cast spells.

We sometimes take on the judgments of others and continue to repeat the lies they told us about ourselves, even if they are no longer in our life. So, please be aware of your inner voice and make sure it is kind, gentle, and encouraging. Push pause on all negative self-talk. Speak to and treat yourself as you would your own best friend. Acknowledge that you are a child of the Universe and, therefore, worthy of all the riches of the kingdom simply because you were born.

As for me, I did not have that understanding, so I did what I had always done, which was to keep plowing forward. Believe me when I say it often felt hard and laborious.

However, I was still determined to create a better life, although I had no idea how to do that. I kept volunteering to assist in personal growth workshops for women, which furthered my own growth. I also started reading inspirational books from authors such as Louise Hay and Wayne Dyer.

I wrote affirmations every day. And after reading *Creative Visualization* by Shakti Gawain on using the power of imagination to create what you want, I started visualizing what I wanted in my life. Without being aware I was doing so, I was tapping into the Law of Attraction.

On the night of September 15, 1992, I attended a BBQ, where I unexpectedly met my now husband. Initially,

I had no intention of going, and I told the hosts that I was definitely not interested in another blind date. Other well-meaning friends had set me up with some "winners." However, they assured me it was just a get-together because Colin, a friend from Australia, was stopping overnight and flying back home the next day. I had not seen them in quite a long time, and they were always fun to visit. So, with the pressure off, I accepted the invitation.

Something extraordinary happened for both Colin and me that night. I wouldn't say it was love at first sight, although I do remember telling a friend that I would certainly date him if he lived here. I laughed more that night than I had in years, and we stayed awake almost all night talking. I felt a pang of disappointment when he left in the morning.

I was surprised to get a call from him about a week later, and once again, we talked like old friends who had known each other for years. That went on for a while. Then, one day, he boldly asked me if I would fly to Australia if he sent me a ticket. I was both excited and terrified of the idea, and I could not give him an answer right away. There were so many considerations: Australia was on the other side of the world, and I knew no one there, I had not known him very long, and what if it did not all go according to plan, and, well, I am sure you can imagine my doubts and fears.

In the end, everything fell into place more easily than anything had ever happened for me in my life. To my surprise, relief, and delight, I had a friend who had a friend in Australia near the town where Colin lived. This person agreed to be my contact, which gave me peace of mind.

My landlord then offered me one month of free rent if I painted my condo. Another dear friend was thrilled to come to stay with my daughter for the two weeks I would be gone. My daughter was eighteen by then and did not need anyone staying with her, but it gave me more peace of mind. One by one, all my considerations were met. Finally, I decided to treat it like a holiday, and I said YES!

Colin then proceeded to sweep me off my feet. In the month that followed, until I was to fly there, he came up with the brilliant idea of using a mini recorder to walk me through the subtropical area of Western Australia where he lived. Day after day, he would record and mail me a tape with his view of the magnificent land that had been his home for twenty years, ever since he left his homeland of Canada. In the telling, he shared himself and who he was to such a degree that I fell in love with him before I ever landed in Perth.

As crazy as it sounds (just as crazy as when we remind each other of the story), he asked me to move in with him the day after I arrived.

In the past, I would have been overjoyed that somebody I was attracted to wanted me; it would have been an instant YES, with the details figured out later. But instead, feeling the way I already did about him, the words, "If I'm not good enough to marry, I'm not good enough to live with," flew out of my mouth. I had done enough personal growth to be clear that the end of my journey was marriage. I knew my vision was to be happily married. I was committed; it was that or nothing.

As I said earlier, I tell every woman I coach, *clarity is power*, and without a clearly defined blueprint, you cannot build your dream. Blueprints are essential to any project as they clearly illustrate the specific vision of the intended result.

At that time, I knew part of my vision, but not all of it. I still had a lot to learn and transform to become the woman I am today. However, at the age of thirty-nine, I did know that I had been hurt way too many times in relationships to settle for anything less than the longing of my heart.

The deal breaker was that I did not want to move to Australia; when he let me know he was ready to move home to Canada, I said YES. We set the wedding date for six months later, with no doubt that he would find work in Canada. It felt like a whirlwind at the time, and when I look back, it was. However, we both agreed that our decision to be together was right in every way.

For the next seven years, I felt like I was on a roller coaster ride. I do not like roller coasters, so I assure you, it tested me a lot. If I had known then what I know now, I would have seen that time in my life as the butterfly's struggle, similar to each of us as spiritual beings having a human experience. Although the human part of us may feel resistance to the growth required for transformation, the divine part beckons us to the next upward spiral of who we are becoming. Our best self.

Colin came over a few weeks before the wedding, intending to land a job. Much to our disappointment, however, he could not find work in his field, no matter how hard he tried. I was devastated, especially when, after all his attempts failed, he announced, "Honey, there is no other option; I have to return to Australia and continue working there." That left me with a monumental decision to make.

I had a dream, and I was in love with it. Sadly, I had no idea how to create it now that Colin was leaving Canada. Regardless, I was unwavering in my desire for a committed relationship and was determined to find the solution, no matter what. It was not easy, and it was not convenient to make a firm decision to stay true to my dream. My belief in either-or rose like a dragon. Either I could move to Australia to live with the love of my life, or I could stay in Canada to be with my family.

After days of talking, trying on ideas, and agonizing about the wisdom of getting married, I conceived a plan. I would move to Australia with Colin and have my two grown children immigrate there to join us; they both thought the idea was an exciting adventure. So that is what I did. In the following long months, I discovered what a lengthy process it was and realized the dream of having my children join us there would not happen.

My son and his partner were expecting their first child. He was establishing himself in Canada as a family man. My daughter did come to join us for a short time. She had her immigration papers; however, she decided it was not her dream to live in Australia, and she returned to Canada.

This turn of events knocked me sideways. I thought I had experienced loss in my life, but nothing prepared me for the moment I realized that I was halfway across the world from my children, who I loved most in the entire Universe. It was heartbreaking when it finally registered; I could not make my dream their dream, and they were not coming to Australia to join my husband and me.

I grieved with a pain so deep it began to crush me. At first, I could not see a way to make it work, a way to be happy. I tortured myself with thoughts like, "Should I stay in Australia with my husband or go back home to be with my family?"

At that time, there was no internet service, therefore no Zoom or FaceTime. And phone calls were prohibitively expensive, limiting how often I could call my children. As a result, I felt utterly disconnected from my family, stuck without a solution, and unbearably trapped.

Has that ever happened to you? Has there been a time you began to wonder if your dream would ever happen, and you felt like I did, completely discouraged?

I flew home for a visit shortly after my grandson, Traimin, was born, and I saw that my adult children were creating their lives; my role as mom had changed. That made me realize I had to find a way to reinvent my life with my husband and also stay connected to my family. In that moment, something reared up in me that shifted my hope for my dream to happen, into a wholehearted, no-matter-what, DESIRE.

Until that shift, I could not see a way, so I had been wavering on myself and my dreams. Since then, I have learned that everything in our life journey is an opportunity for growth and evolution. Did I dig deeper to find a way? You bet I did! As Napoleon Hill said, "Dreams are not born of indifference, laziness, or lack of ambition."

My thinking took a new turn, and I ultimately came up with a fabulous idea. My first splendid goal was to fly home every six to eight months and stay for three weeks at a time to saturate myself in connection with my family, my grown children, and my very first grandchild, my amazing grandson, Traimin.

To accomplish that, I first had to find a way to make more money. The flight was over two thousand dollars. Immediately more ideas appeared the minute I started to focus on that plan and commit to it with all my heart as a starting point to the solution. My next brilliant thought was to sell the one expensive piece of jewelry I owned that had no other purpose and use it to take my next trip to Canada. It worked! I felt free!

Once I tasted the choices that extra money could afford me, I was on fire to create enough wealth to have total freedom. The purpose of my sole focus was to create a financial foundation of security with an amount that allowed us to semi-retire and move home to Canada. It was a burning desire, and I do mean burning-desire vision. Catherine Ponder, the world-renowned author and prosperity lecturer, writes in her book *Dynamic Laws of Prosperity*, "There is nothing weak or lukewarm about true desire. It is intense and powerful. If properly developed and expressed, a strong desire also carries with it the power for success."

I have always known the power of taking action. It is not enough to dream, set intentions, and visualize; **you must take action.** In *The Science of Getting Rich,* Wallace Wattles writes, "By thought the thing you want is brought to you; by action you receive it." Action provides a channel for the Law of Attraction.

It was not really about the money; it was the freedom that the money gave me. As a result of that all-consuming desire, I discovered an entrepreneurial tendency that sparked new possibilities and eventually led to an abundance of ideas and opportunities that I would never have dreamt would occur or come my way.

I will share the details as we continue our journey together. Please know, though, that in the end, it doesn't really matter what ideas came to me to fulfill my burning desire because yours will be unique to you. There is not a one-size-fits-all idea in the Master Game of Life.

Who could have imagined that after being laid off from a good-paying job right before I met the man of my dreams, he would send me a ticket to fly to Australia that I was free to accept? Who would have thought I would discover I had a knack for renovating homes and selling them for a profit? Who would have guessed that I would be passionate about selling advertising for a newspaper and helping businesses grow, increasing my net worth? How could I possibly have predicted that I would meet an advertising client in the banking industry who showed me the perfect Term Deposits in which to invest? Who knew my husband would love it enough to join me in the new venture?

What a surprise that we both felt it was an adventure to live as minimalists while building the dream together! An even greater surprise was to find out he had his own dream of becoming a millionaire. How had we not ever talked about this vision? That is what I call a synchronistic phenomenon. My clients and I often marvel about such experiences and our favorite expression is, "You can't make this up!"

Pain pushed me until this expanded vision, fueled by my passionate desire, pulled me. Day after day, running on the sandy Australian shore of the magnificent Indian Ocean, I felt exalted and excited, dancing with my dream! And in August 2000, my dream was realized when Colin and I moved home to Canada and began the next phase of our journey.

Key #5
Bridge the Gap

I am celebrating you for reaching this point in the journey of creating your dream life by envisioning and naming the yearnings and longings you sense are bigger possibilities for you. This action opens up an expanded space for you to grow into and become the woman you have always felt is your highest potential.

Listening to your soul's hunger ignites the burning desire we spoke of in Key #4. However, staying tapped into that feeling can be a little more challenging.

In Key #5, we put another powerful piece of the puzzle in place. Are you ready for liberation? Find a nice comfy spot where you will not be disturbed while you discover how to overcome any obstacles on the path between where you are right now and where you deeply desire to be in your future.

When we commit to creating a life we yearn for, we can attract and generate the resources to thrive. That is because our higher power—the Infinite—ALSO wants those results through us. We are part of a bigger picture.

I have seen some amazing results happen for my clients once they claim their spot to create their dream life. For example, one of my clients, Kristin, a successful lawyer in the Okanagan, received an unexpected bonus at work right after she began the DreamBuilder Program. I tell my clients not to be surprised when these wins come *out of the blue*; do expect to be amazed!

Another client, Tarryn Hamilton, an acclaimed realtor in Calgary, Alberta, made the largest commission of her career shortly after we started working together. She easily created that outstanding result while following her heart's calling to be at home more often with her young children. As a result, Tarryn spent more time with her family than ever before while, at the same time, breaking through the ceiling of her multi-six-figure business by 40% over ten months. What is noteworthy is that she held fast to her desire as a mom to spend more quality time with her children while at the same time staying true to her passion and values of giving 100% first-class service to her clients so they reach their real estate goals and dreams.

However, it is essential to be aware of something else that happens when we are courageous enough to declare what we would love and decide to go for it.

When we decide to do something new, every belief that differs will get stirred up and cause feelings of uncertainty, resistance, or fear. Then as we begin to move forward, we bump into these inner obstacles.

These hidden barriers are in the GAP between where we are right now and the life we sense, dream, and sometimes pray is possible for us. They take us into an old story about who we are and what is within the realms of possibility for us.

We all have well-known stories we tell ourselves, and often others, about why we do not have the life we yearn for—stories we compose from our life experiences, personal history, and who or what is responsible.

I reassure you that as we create a vision and begin taking steps toward that new life, it is normal for our old life to exert a gravitational pull back to the familiar.

It is not IF it will happen; it is WHEN it will happen. Our dream calls us to step out of our comfort zone, away from our well-known routines. That is where the magic happens and we sky rocket our success!

The invisible inner barrier that stops us is who we believe we are or are not. When we cannot create the life we long for in one or more areas, we subconsciously interpret it to mean that we are not enough in some way, something is wrong with us, or that it is possible for others but not for us.

We feel powerless in the gap. Until we identify our patterns of stuckness, we stay powerless, straddled between what we deeply desire and the doubt that we will ever attain it. As it takes grit and grace to look at what is in the gap, I have devoted two Keys to help you transform and release whatever you discover, so you can reclaim your power and step into your greatness.

My client, Dr. Hoda Hosseini, a successful periodontist in Winnipeg, Manitoba, is happier than she has ever been and loves her life these days. In a beautiful video recording, she tells this story after completing the DreamBuilder Program with me.

"For thirty-five years, my mind had trained only in logic and scientific thinking. My focus was only on my career and continued professional climb in the past ten years. I worked hard, and although, by any standard, you would call me a success, I did not feel I was. I had a beautiful and loving family, a fantastic and thriving business, and a welcoming community, yet I felt something was missing. I had deep anxiety about not being enough and not doing enough. I continually compared myself with those around me, and in my mind, I always came up short. I never celebrated any achievement and continually criticized what I perceived to be my shortcomings."

Scan the QR Code with your smart phone to hear Dr. Hoda Hosseini's testimonial or go to: https://youtu.be/AnnzXA8ok6M

Do you recognize yourself in Hoda's story? No matter how much you have done or accomplished, you may still feel that you are not enough or have not done enough. This erroneous feeling comes from deep within our earlier conditioning, also known as our PARADIGMS.

When we do not have the support or skills to shift out of our stories, it gets uncomfortable, and we continue to retreat into our current life patterns, even if it is not what we enjoy. When we live this way—by default—we run on autopilot, with only fleeting bursts of inspiration and passion. And therefore, we continue to get the same results over and over again.

What gets in our way is not something outside of ourselves. It is not the economy, where we live, how educated we are, or any external reason we think it might be. Instead, our paradigms cause this dissonance we experience at times. The limitation is never "out there"; it is always inside us.

Paradigms are patterns of thoughts that run in the background of our minds. They influence our beliefs, feelings, and actions and therefore cause the results we get. They stem from old beliefs that we acquire in childhood. They then become fear-based habits that protect the status quo.

When the voice of fear is louder than our positive mindset voice of "I can do this," which feels unfamiliar and uncomfortable, we often give in to that fear. Then we abandon our dreams, and sometimes ourselves.

Have you heard from your paradigms since you started thinking about your dreams and writing a vision for a life you would love? If you have, you are not alone. That internal voice of fear, doubt, and worry—your paradigm—is programmed to keep everything the same as it has always been.

I am shining a very bright light on this point for a reason. The truth is, when a paradigm shows up, it is GOOD NEWS!

Your paradigm will not show up when you are in your comfort zone, not growing, not trying anything new, or hesitating to reach for a higher level of success. When you feel that conflict, discomfort, or fear trying to pull you back to the familiar, it means you are on a growth track, which is great!

The resistance we experience shuts down many women's dreams before they ever have a chance to take any action. We do that in many perverse ways. We put the brakes on our internal power, withhold our love and energy, or we procrastinate. As you read these words, do they resonate as truth for you? Can you identify ways you have shut down that could stop your progression?

I know firsthand that our inner voice sometimes feels like a loud, relentlessly critical message telling us to give up or a warning that we are failing.

My paradigms are often very nasty and try to make me give up. For instance, when it came time to write my story for this book, thoughts like these attacked me: "Are you crazy, telling the whole world your stories of failure? People will surely reject you once they find out who you really are. You are making a total fool out of yourself. Nobody wants to hear about you; you are not important." And on and on AND ON it goes, at times.

If you have a similarly loud voice making it hard for you to believe there is a chance for you to manifest your dreams, perhaps you and I are in each other's lives for a reason. Consider that discovering this new way of creating whatever you love might be that reason.

I invite you to set an intention to become aware of these paradigms so you will recognize them when they show up. I encourage you to be even more determined to align with your vision and the future you are committed to creating.

The paradigm shows up in three ways. We call them the 3Ds in the DreamBuilder Program.

The first D stands for Delay, also known as distraction. Let's say I have decided to do a Facebook live to promote a workshop I am doing. Then I think I should first clean my office before I do it. Then I think, perhaps I will do it tomorrow because now I am a bit tired and won't be at my best.

The second D is Dissuasion. I tell myself I tried doing a Facebook live promo last week, but as I do not see results, it's probably not worth the effort.

The third D is Defcon, when we feel a sense of fear and anxiety, sometimes with physical symptoms like nausea, stomach pain, headaches, or trembling. Our hearts can beat faster; from experience, I can assure you that it's even scarier once we reach a certain age.

If we listen to the voice of our paradigms and feel these symptoms, it can lead to giving up on our dream altogether.

Every one of us has acquired beliefs and patterns of behavior that can limit us from reaching our full potential. A higher part of us (our true nature) wants to live a freer, fuller, more expansive life, and another, smaller part of us (our ego) wants to stay in our comfort zone. These paradigms are in the gap between where we are and the results we crave.

When you identify these paradigms and use them as opportunities instead of allowing them to stop you, it means you are growing and shifting results in your life. Even if you are wildly successful, there is always a higher level of extraordinary results possible for you.

Our paradigms act like an internal thermostatic setting in all aspects of our life. Whatever is occurring in our external world has everything to do with what is happening inside us. When your subconscious beliefs or feelings do not align with your aspirations, you have internal emotional struggles, and self-sabotage is common.

Our current results are a perfect outer reflection of our inner paradigms. For example, let's say you would like to make more money. Consciously, you think doubling your income would be a good thing and would make you happy. However, you feel uncomfortable whenever you visualize yourself with that higher income.

You may find yourself having thoughts like, "It will never happen. That's way too much. I would have to work too hard. That's impossible. I can't do that on my own. And besides, I would have to pay more taxes anyway."

The idea of wanting to double our current income while having opposing thoughts or feelings about our ability to do so is a perfect example of the thoughts that lead to the results we do or do not manifest. Part of us loves the idea of more money, while the other part gets very specific in the messages that cause resistance.

There was a time before I knew about this dichotomy when I would beat myself up whenever my behavior was not aligned with what I said I wanted. I was unaware of the story I was repeatedly telling myself. I focused on the negative as I had done my entire life because I thought the way I was trained to think. I would not praise myself, no matter how amazing of a job I did. Instead, I would see the one aspect I had done wrong or could have done better.

For example, I would see a speck of lint on the freshly vacuumed carpet out of the corner of my eye and then proceed to re-vacuum the whole living room until it was perfect. Just ask my kids. No one was allowed to step in the room for fear it would mess up the shadow carpets and ruin my carefully crafted illusion of perfection.

I did not realize these very thoughts were directly responsible for perpetuating the problems I had. I truly believed the conditions of my life were the issue, and if only they would change, then I would be happy.

All of these behaviors resulted from the belief that I was not good enough. If my house was not perfect, I did not measure up as a wife and mother. The same impossibly high standards applied to my body as a woman. In my mind, anything less than perfection meant I was not good enough.

If I had known then what I know now, I would have understood that our thoughts and beliefs become our reality. So eventually, as you know, I found myself living out these beliefs in my lifestyle. I was twice divorced, living in that rented basement suite in East Vancouver, stretching my paycheck to make ends meet.

The subconscious mind has no sense of humor or ability for inductive reasoning. It does not know the difference between reality and fantasy. It simply believes what the conscious mind is telling it. We cannot have thoughts of lack and limitation and expect the abundance we desire.

Emerson stated, "Stand guard at the portal of your mind."

When I invested in myself and my future with coaching and mentoring from successful women who had a higher level of awareness than I did, I became aware of my thoughts. I learned to question my beliefs about myself and how the world worked.

There was tremendous power in waking up to what was causing the conditions in my life. I was no longer at the effect of my circumstances. I broke free, claiming my sovereignty. It is my greatest intention for every woman I support and coach to do the same.

My joint venture partner, Brenda Jungwirth, and I have created a program, Women In Dentistry, to empower women in the dental field. One of our clients, Dr. Krystal Hakkaart, is running two successful practices in British Columbia, Canada; Elevate Dental in Vernon and Apple Creek Family Dental in Armstrong.

During our coaching sessions, Krystal became aware that her paradigms were keeping her in an old story, causing her to spiral and sending her down a rabbit hole of negativity whenever she faced a challenge in one of her clinics.

However, with the tools and strategies Krystal learned in our Women In Dentistry program, she now recognizes when she is getting pulled into an old belief and quickly pivots to shift into positive solutions.

Krystal has always been a gifted and skillful dentist; however, running a successful dental practice, much less two, requires another expertise. As she has gained mastery in her mindset, Krystal has acquired the leadership skills to increase productivity and accelerate the growth of her two thriving clinics. Among the wins she now celebrates are happier staff, improved office morale, and her patients receiving the client-focused, gentle care that ensures visiting the dentist is a positive experience—fulfilling Krystal's mission and passion.

I tell my clients that we grow and expand when supported and championed. When we are isolated, we have only ourselves to listen to; therefore, the level of success we believe is possible is determined solely by the stories we tell ourselves. You have a vision of what you would love to accomplish, and NOW is your time!

Key #6

Befriend Your Fear

When we decide on a dream, there is a part of us that unequivocally says "YES!" And yet, a part of us remains resistant and reacts by summoning old, familiar stories in an attempt to hold us back. *This* is the voice of fear, doubt, anxiety, and at times even terror, fostered from our unconscious paradigms—as we discovered in Key #5.

**To master the results we desire,
we must "befriend our fear."**

When we recognize how our fear shows up and learn how to manage it when it does, we start to hear the powerful messages behind it.

Fear does not mean we *cannot* create what we want; it simply tells us we have not done it *yet*. It informs us we are about to make bold moves, actions we have not taken before.

Greatness includes some fear, and we can embrace it as a stepping-stone to creating and living a life beyond our wildest dreams! What does it mean to make friends with fear?

It is learning to view your fear as feedback, alerting you when you push past your comfort zone toward a path of growth and using it as an opportunity to break through the barriers that keep you from soaring. It is all right to have some fear; however, do NOT let fear have you!

We often experience fear when trying something new or going to a place we have not yet been in our lives. When those fears emerge, they can hypnotize us into a state of powerlessness which, if given into, can completely immobilize us, and keeps us grinding our way through life or giving up altogether.

I watched the demise of my mother—a woman who lost herself because she felt powerless, beaten down, and demoralized by a life she hated. Discouraged and disheartened, she eventually lost all hope. It was excruciatingly heartbreaking to witness. Sadly, she never reached her full potential and passed away too early.

My mother was and still is a big motivation for immersing myself in the field of personal growth. As much as I loved her, I was determined not to follow in her footsteps.

Yet I found myself living at the same level of unhappiness. Even though our circumstances differed, I somehow repeated my mom's behaviors, beliefs, and actions. And I was passing that legacy on to my children. Once conscious of that, I made a silent pledge deep within myself that I would break the cycle. I refused to pass this dysfunctional pattern down to my family.

It was a generational cycle from which I first had to break free. From everything I have studied, I believe that whatever has affected one generation without full resolution is passed on to the next one. With this new understanding, my heart goes out to my mom, as I now know it didn't start with her but began generations before. Living two doors away from my grandparents and witnessing the hostility, on top of hearing the stories about my mother's upbringing, left me with no misconceptions about the offensive manner in which she was raised. I was determined to transform the generational pattern from disempowerment, drama, and disparagement into strength, sovereignty, and salvation.

I have since discovered how to attain freedom, and everything I have learned I now offer to all women who are highly motivated to achieve lasting change.

Developing the resources needed to remain steady in your conviction to manifest your dreams is vital, even more so when those fears show up. Let's look at how to use your fear as an opportunity for expansion and transformation.

YOU are the designer of your life. The pen is in your hand. Whatever you have the impulse to *Be, Do, or Have,* is possible! Women all over the world are awakening to a new stage of evolution. There has never been a more momentous time in history to expand and express the highest possibilities of who we are.

Many people experience fear when faced with the seemingly impossible—even the most accomplished among us. However, successful people do not let fear make their decisions. Instead, they focus on what is possible. Fear is simply a made-up story, one that does not exist. So, decide to focus on POSSIBILITY!

Have you ever had a failure in your life? We ALL have! It might have been when we were learning to walk or to talk, eat food on our own, dress, or tie our shoelaces. We all failed a few times before we succeeded.

When we befriend our fear, we permit ourselves to fail often enough to achieve success. We keep trying again and again—and again! We learned to walk by falling, to talk by saying unintelligible words, and to feed ourselves by dropping food everywhere first. As adults, we stop giving ourselves permission to fail, condemning ourselves when we do not get it perfect the first time we try. Instead, we persist in working harder and harder to prove ourselves; or give up altogether.

If our company is not thriving, we might think, "I guess I am not meant to run a business." If we experience a broken relationship, we may say, "I guess love is not in the cards for me," or "Maybe there is something wrong with me."

And if we have a belief system that has governed the way we experience lack in our life, especially the absence of financial abundance, we may think, "I don't deserve it because I don't work hard enough." Another common belief is "I came from a poor family," or "It's impossible to get ahead because everything is so expensive." Or perhaps, "Wealth is for others, not for me. Besides, I've always been bad at math and have never understood how money works!"

When the skeptical inner voice of uncertainty deceives us with a story that we are not good enough, we are prone to giving up on ourselves. Instead of plugging into our power confidently, we imagine all the obstacles in our way. As a result, we often give in to our fear-driven beliefs, which become our walking, breathing identity, and we feel powerless to reach our dreams.

Pause to remember the book title: **Never Ever Give Up!**

Too often, I have quit on myself and my dreams, succumbing to shameful memories of my mistakes. I felt enslaved by the relentless echoes of a lifetime of failures, haunted by the price I had paid for my poor choices and the cost to those I cared about. I wanted to show up and shine, but the wounds of my past overshadowed me.

My experience as the new girl in grade six in that small-town school, where children bullied me for years, created a belief that told me it was not safe to show up. My fear said, "Dim your light, do not draw attention to yourself, play small and stay safe or you will be hurt again." My fear still tries to hold me back with that same misguided message.

Our comfort zone is an illusion. Yet, we try to protect that space by avoiding uncomfortable change and keeping our lives static. The fact of life is that everything is constantly changing. Day becomes night, and night becomes day. Seasons change, and our bodies change. Nothing is permanent. The idea of a safe place where nothing changes is a delusion.

Have you ever given up when a paradigm crept in and told you that you would not survive if you took a risk?

That is the voice of **F**alse **E**vidence **A**ppearing **R**eal (F.E.A.R.). It is the part of you that does not like change and will do whatever it can to remain the same. It is like the border patrol standing guard at the edge of your comfort zone, keeping you anchored in the familiar past with predictable outcomes.

Fear often hides behind your limiting beliefs, unconscious patterns, and paradigms. It will not say, "I am here to kill your dreams." Fear is too smart for that, often disguising itself as practicality. The voice of reason warns, "Now is not a good time. Wait until later." It cautions, "You don't have the money for that anyway. That is irresponsible."

Fear can also take the tone of a guardian, protecting you by promising, "I am here to keep you safe. Remember that time you made a fool of yourself? I am here to save you from getting embarrassed or rejected, so you never have to experience that level of pain again."

While it can be wise to heed the voice of caution, fear can also cause confusion, making it hard to trust our gut instinct—our sage internal guidance system. For this reason, many women ask me how to distinguish whether their thoughts and feelings are intuition or fear. That is a GREAT question!

Our superpower of intuition is one worth studying and getting to know. We are all connected to intuition—an infinite intelligence bigger than our minds that we tap into through deep wisdom. Many of us are unknowingly disconnected from the gift that is our spiritual guidance system, which is why we have challenges distinguishing if the messages we receive are inspired insights or fear-based.

So how do you know if it is best to proceed? Begin by noticing whether the message you hear makes you feel *contractive* or *expansive*. When facing a choice or making a decision, which option makes you feel stressed in any way? And which makes you feel lighter, more energized, more hopeful?

These feelings feed you essential information. Yet, the logical mind often tries to override this higher internal guidance. If you do not trust your feelings or have disconnected from them altogether, it is hard to determine whether the message is coming from the part of you that wants to protect you at all costs or from your inner voice of truth.

One way to determine if a thought, hunch, or gut feeling is fear or intuition is to see if you feel agitated. Fear has a distinct tone of panic or frenzy, often making you feel bad about yourself or the situation. On the other hand, when a message comes from your intuition, it is carried with feelings of calm, peace, and an overriding knowing that this is your higher wisdom speaking. In other words, you will not be distraught when you hear it.

I have heard it said on more than one occasion that the voice of truth is only as loud as our willingness to listen. In *Dynamic Laws of Prosperity*, Catherine Ponder says, "People whom the world considers to be of genius caliber are those who have had the courage and confidence to listen to and follow the guidance of their intuition and creative imagination."

The degree to which we access our intuition is determined by our willingness to hear, trust, and pay attention to it. We connect to a power that knows how to overcome any challenges and help us manifest our dreams.

Albert Einstein said, "The intuitive mind is a sacred gift, and the rational mind is a faithful servant. We have created a society that honors the servant and has forgotten the gift."

Culturally, women have been trained not to trust our inner wisdom but instead to rely on logic. We have been raised in a masculine model of reasoning and thinking versus trusting our feelings and intuition.

I am eternally grateful for the committed women who diligently help liberate and encourage us to embrace our feminine power. Studying the Feminine Power course with Dr. Claire Zammit has been a richly rewarding experience as a participant and a transformational coach.

We often get stuck in a loop in our minds trying to figure out how to manifest our dreams. We cannot create from just our minds alone. We must feel spiritually connected, attuned to our inner power, to become the woman we were born to be. Form an unshakable bond with your higher power to access your internal guidance system.

Fear takes us out of our inner wisdom and into our heads. Dr. Daniel Amen speaks about intuition in his book, *Unleash the Power of the Female Brain,* calling it one of our strongest assets. He claims that women tap more into the right side of the brain, which is considered the seat of the emotional and spiritual worlds.

Our brain has two hemispheres. The right hemisphere houses the subconscious. Functioning intuitively, it integrates information gathered through our senses, pictures, and other non-verbal means; it stores and processes in a complex, multi-dimensional system. The left side holds conscious thought and operates in an analytical, logical, detail-oriented, linear fashion.

It makes sense that our conscious minds can quickly grasp why the fear of an unknown future causes hesitation and our past failures and perceived shortcomings can stop us from moving forward. However, sometimes it is generated, as it was for me, from trauma.

We think of traumatic events as accidents, violent crimes, natural disasters, or obvious traumas like abuse, neglect, and abandonment. However, ordinary day-to-day events can also create the same trauma response in both the mind and body.

Examples can include betrayal, losing a job, rejection, financial loss, or the death of a loved one. For children, these painful incidents might involve being laughed at or ignored by their peers, spoken to harshly by a parent or teacher, or told they are too loud, lazy, or stupid.

The experience can be daunting, whether from past trauma or repeated painful experiences. We then develop coping behaviors to protect, defend, or prove ourselves. Or we play small and hide instead of pursuing our dreams and the success we desire.

Trauma is unresolved pain that buzzes like background static in our lives, affecting our nervous system and influencing our actions and reactions. Whether we remember the traumatic incident or something in our unconscious is triggered, we fear it might happen again, activating our survival instincts.

This response is a programmed brain function that triggers our nervous system and floods our body with chemicals so that we can do whatever it takes to survive any danger—our fight, flight, or freeze response. Our primary wiring is designed to help us defend ourselves, run away from perceived danger, or freeze—rendering us incapable of taking action.

Understanding that our autonomic nervous system kicks into action, causing physical symptoms when we are fearful, has greatly benefited me. Several times in my earlier life, my common reaction to something I perceived as a threat was to freeze. Through my extensive training, I learned to recognize what was happening to me.

We are hardwired for survival, so our nervous system does not recognize the difference between a present-day fear, like doing a live post on social media, or a saber-tooth tiger tracking us for its next meal. As a result, it does not distinguish between taking our business to the next level and asking for a sale or contracting COVID.

I have gained valuable awareness working with my coach at Brave Thinking Institute, Kirsten Welles, an expert in the field of energy medicine and a Doctor of Traditional Chinese Medicine. Once I learned how to calm my overstimulated nervous system, I had a reawakening and found a connection with myself that prevented fear from keeping me stuck. However, these automatic reactions do not dissipate on their own. We must do the work to heal and transform whatever is holding us back.

In the same way, when we continue living in anxiety, replaying a past trauma, or telling the story our mind created—about other people, ourselves, and the world— we continue to hardwire the trauma response in our body. As discussed in Key #5, our mind creates these stories to protect us from experiencing the same pain. However, it also instills limiting beliefs that cause fear. So, we keep living out these stories and thus repeating similar events.

Imagine a child who gets into trouble every time they do something that displeases a parent, like accidentally spilling milk at the table or not cleaning their room to a high enough standard. That child may believe that they have to be good, or even perfect, to be loved and treated well. Unless they change those thoughts dictating the need to behave to be liked, loved, and accepted, they will most likely become a people pleaser, conversely rebellious, or even freeze in situations that scare them.

For many years, I lived primarily in the fight, flight, or freeze reactive mode, never realizing this was not normal—those fear-based reactions are usually temporary, alerting us to danger. Then, we go back to rest and digest once the danger passes. That is how our nervous system maintains healthy regulation—so remaining in fear hinders our ability to be the best version of ourselves.

The first thing I do to interrupt my powerless energetic state is to move my body. Whether in that immobilized condition or fight mode, I start by breathing as deeply as I can in the moment. I have learned that I need to move my energy with deep breathing. Have you ever noticed that you take shallow breaths or stop breathing when you are stressed?

The best breathing technique I know is one I learned from my preeminent coach, Kirsten, and is the principal tool I use when I am feeling stressed or anxious. We breathe a few times—in through our nose and out of our mouth like we are blowing out of a straw. This breath calms our nervous system, and we can begin to think more clearly when we relax our nervous system. Then we can make a move.

Depending on my situation, I will walk around the block, put on some music, do some yoga, and truly get into my body. I choose whatever will reorient and ground me. When we are grounded, we can expand our energy rather than feel contracted or shrinking.

Do you find yourself becoming dysregulated in certain situations and relationships? Do you think you do not have the mental, emotional, or spiritual capacity to show up in your life as the woman you long to be? If so, it may benefit you to ask yourself if you have unresolved trauma.

If you know or suspect you have experienced trauma, I strongly encourage you to seek the services of a professional to help you release and heal whatever is there for you. There are many effective therapies available to us today. I would highly recommend looking into EFT/Tapping (Emotional Freedom Techniques) and EMDR Therapy (Eye Movement Desensitization and Reprocessing). Both techniques have aided me greatly in experiencing profound healing.

What you have experienced matters—resolving trauma allows us to live as the best version of ourselves. I used to judge myself for not getting over the events of my past that hurt me. However, I have come to believe that this attitude makes our journey to recovery much more challenging, and it takes longer.

Do not do what I did for years, telling myself it was no big deal; so many others had it much worse than I did, and I should just get over it and move on. I found it difficult to acknowledge what had happened, be true to myself, and offer myself the same compassion or empathy I would always provide others. No wonder creating a successful and healthy life for myself was arduous.

I discovered that when I gave myself the grace to acknowledge my painful experiences without letting them define me, I could heal and choose a new story to guide me into my future. It set me free!

Once I released the emotional charge from my more painful encounters, I was then able to notice my familiar fear intensifying when I chose to try something new. I felt empowered by thanking my fear for alerting me that I was on a growth path!

That is possible for all of us when we have the courage to shine the light on unhealed wounds and uncried tears. However, I do not believe anyone heals their trauma alone. We cannot become our best selves on our own. We need allies and support to evolve into our highest potential.

I utilize many awareness exercises in my deeper transformational breakthrough workshops. I believe there are parts of us that do not get enough light, which is why we do not shine.

There is no such thing as shallow transformation. Disruption and discomfort are necessary ingredients for change. Let me know if you are motivated to move past your inner blocks, excuses, limiting beliefs, and circumstances. We can talk about the next intimate, up-close, life-changing workshop adventure for sheroes.

Our most painful experiences are often the catalysts for our growth and evolution. In Key #3, I mentioned Standing Firm When Your World Is Shaking. In that program, we learn that despite what has happened, we can use the experience to become a better version of ourselves and transform our lives.

When I was away in the Bahamas on a business trip, I contracted COVID. I had that same earlier fear response. First, anxiety flooded my body, and I panicked, and then I froze. With the seminar now over and being so far from home, unable to board the flight back to Canada made me feel helpless. I sat staring out the condo window for over an hour. I felt paralyzed and could not formulate a coherent thought about what action to take, alone in a foreign country.

I knew I had to move from the condo because the new rental guests were arriving soon. Still, I remained immobile. I was terrified. As the time got closer to leaving the room, it was only the clock that catapulted me out of my frozen state and into action. I had the tools that could have freed me much earlier than the dictates of that ticking clock. Nevertheless, fear temporarily seduced me into an earlier pattern.

Years ago, these reactive patterns were how I walked through life. Today, by using my learned tools, I can get myself out of such a state in hours instead of being numb for days, sometimes weeks at a time.

I started by breathing deeply and feeling my breath in my body, and then I practiced some EFT on myself and did my calming breath sequence. Once I relaxed into accepting that an extended stay in the Bahamas was happening, I utilized one of the most powerful aspects of the Standing Firm When Your World is Shaking program: finding a way to relate to a challenging situation in an empowering way. From there, I declared to myself that I would find and embrace the gift this experience came to give me.

I focused my attention inward, deeply connecting with the infinite and my intuition, using it as a growth opportunity. Finally, it occurred to me that I needed to be away from my daily life with all the demands and distractions of my busy schedule to have an intimate conversation with my dreams.

I had been living in fear of COVID since it started, and I was astonished to realize I had unconsciously put a lid on picturing myself far in the future. Instead, I had been playing small and not dreaming of what else might be even more potent than this level of success I had already created.

When I woke up to that realization, I knew one of the gifts buried in this experience was taking this unexpected time to recalibrate my dreams and the vision I have for my life to fulfill my purpose with the greatest impact possible.

Staring at the coastline of the Atlantic Ocean in Nassau, I began to imagine myself twenty years from now, vibrantly healthy, dynamically fulfilling my purpose, surrounded by the people I love. And I am on FIRE for this vision!

Mary Morrissey offers this sage wisdom in the book, *Trauma: Healing Your Past to Find Freedom Now*, where Pedram Shojai and Nick Polizzi quote her as saying,

> We can choose to see trauma either as empow-ering or disempowering. The meaning we make of it, the perspective we bring, will either be life giving or life draining. No matter what the trauma has been, no matter how difficult or how long it's been there, with some support we have the ability in us to transform our experience, not of what happened, but of our future life.

One of the ways that fear shows up for women is the paralysis they experience when even thinking about speaking in public. Another is the anxiety that can happen when speaking their truth in personal relationships.

I lost my voice growing up, and I believe many women have lost their voice throughout history, both personally and collectively. Fear of speaking up stifles women to this day.

As I previously stated, losing our voice early in life due to traumatic events and experiences or conditioning that leave us feeling insecure about ourselves can make it challenging to be assertive and authentic. As a result, we can feel blocked, which impacts our ability to say what we want to communicate.

An online self-study course I offer for women addresses the fear of showing up and using our voices and teaches powerful solutions to move beyond it. To create this program, I joined forces with Katie Walker from Perth, Australia, an expert EFT/Tapping Practitioner, to produce Breakthrough 2 (To) Fearless Speaking. It has been a project of love for both of us, teaching women how to clarify their vision, unleash their voice, shine in the world, and step into their greatness.

One of the main ingredients for the success of this program is, in addition to helping you understand how to transform fears when speaking up, we use EFT/Tapping, which involves tapping on acupressure points on the face and upper body. It is a powerful holistic healing method based on the combined principles of ancient Chinese acupressure and modern psychology.

With EFT, we tune in to the negative emotions, feelings, thoughts, and beliefs from experiences and troubling events. Then, we *tap* on specific acupressure points, which releases the energy disruption in the body. As a result, we eliminate negative emotions, feelings, and repetitive, unwanted behaviors. We create an uplifted emotional state that positively impacts our emotional and mental well-being and elevates our perspective. As a result, we see things through a new lens, helping us to achieve our desired goals.

The purpose and aim are to find relief and calm our nervous system to promote healing around the emotional or physical issues that hold us back. In the Fearless Speaking program, we address the emotional issues holding you back from using your powerful voice and shining in the way you want to in your business or personal life.

Once all the stress has left the body, our perception changes, and the way we see things is more positive. It is far easier to manifest our vision when we are in this state, and the outcomes are profound.

EFT improves self-esteem, confidence, and resilience, as it empowers you to take charge of your emotional well-being. Tapping regulates our nervous system by putting our body where it naturally should be, into a state of calmness and equilibrium. As a result, we feel grounded and clear and can gain self-mastery.

What I find most exciting is that we can learn to do EFT on our own once we are taught the pressure points. Then, we can return to a relaxed and grounded state in a short time (sometimes even minutes).

I have seen breakthrough after breakthrough in my clients when we have used the tool of EFT. It is a powerful technique supporting us in creating the changes we desire by clearing stuck energy in our bodies.

I have revolutionized my life by healing old wounds and harnessing my untapped power in the space of trained facilitators of transformation, which is why I now offer the same depth of work. My Breakthrough Retreat is for women who are highly motivated to transform limiting beliefs and release inner blocks to manifest their hearts' desires.

Experiencing my release from trauma is also why I share my journey, mistakes, trials, triumphs, and many of the strategies I have learned along the way that have profoundly and positively affected my life. Everything I share has influenced my life's mission to empower women by using the same methodologies that have helped me flourish.

So, when we hear that voice that wants us to play small, how do we give power to that part of us that wants to move forward and create what we long for; a life filled with joy, satisfaction, purpose, and fulfillment?

When you notice your fears and paradigms showing up, in whatever forms they do, and you start thinking small or trying to talk yourself out of something, here is what you do: Interrupt those thoughts by taking a deep breath and saying out loud, **"Not today!"** For emphasis, you can even stand up and stomp your foot, so your subconscious *really* gets the message. That is what I do! Then focus on the positive vision you have for your life. Re-read what you wrote in your vision statement in Key #2. That vision is your guiding light. Your North Star!

When we give in to fear, we sabotage our greatest dreams. The essential component is a crystal-clear blueprint to stay focused on and connected to our dreams. In this way, you perpetuate the vivid image of yourself as the woman you sense is possible; fully-expressed, vibrant, and living life aligned with who you truly were born to be! Stoking the fire of your desires gives them the power to become your reality.

If you have yet to take that crucial step of writing a vision, pick up your pen, open your journal, and take some time to record your soul's whispers and yearnings. The clearer your vision, the more power it has to become your reality. Listen to the messages of your heart. How does it feel? You have dreams, and they matter! Write them down!

Do not let fear stop you! Instead, let it motivate you.

When you change how you perceive fear, you go from powerless to powerFULL.

Imagine what you could do if you begin to see that the things you are afraid of are nothing more than illusions. What if you stop holding your fear as truth and instead use it as an opportunity to build your resilience and become stronger in your faith?

How big would you play in life? What would you try? What would you do? And the bigger question is, how would the world benefit because of who you have decided to be? How would the world be a better place to live in because fear didn't keep you from holding back your talents, gifts, and expertise?

What if I told you that you do not have to wait for the fear to leave? What if I said that when you get in action, the fear will dissipate into what it always was—nothingness? How would you be different?

These questions are not for your comfort; I ask these questions for your breakthrough.

You are not a prisoner of your past. You have not been sentenced to your story. It is time to disrupt any part of you that allows fear to thwart your glorious future. When you reduce negative emotions of fear, whether from trauma or painful experiences, and change your limiting beliefs to empowering ones, the outcomes will astound you!

I firmly believe in pulling out all stops to support us in creating our desired results. In my experience, there is no such thing as one-size-fits-all. We are talking about the quality of our lives here—our one precious life.

One of the best ways to navigate our way to the higher vision we have for our life is to study successful people, follow them, work with them, and pick up the clues they leave behind.

Successful people are willing to fail and rise again. Oprah Winfrey was fired by television executives and told that she was not fit for TV. We all know she didn't stop with their opinion of her. No, she continued going on to create her studio and become an icon for success worldwide!

The founder of Starbucks, Howard Schultz, was told there was no market for his kind of coffee. His loan application was rejected countless times. According to a report in November 2021, Starbucks had over 33,000 Starbucks stores in eighty countries. Walt Disney was fired from his job at a newspaper for "lacking imagination," which led to the Disney empire.

All of the people in these great success stories have also experienced failure. I have heard over and over that fear and failure are prerequisites for achieving great dreams.

"Think like a queen. A queen is not afraid to fail. Failure is another stepping-stone to greatness."
—Oprah Winfrey

So, when the voice of fear questions you, "What if you fail?" let your response be, "Bring it on! If I fail, I will rise up, keep going, and I *will* succeed!"

Once you are aware of what has subconsciously been going on that has kept you from attaining the results you would love, you then have the power to make a change.

You cannot change your paradigms from the sidelines. The only place to shift them is when you are in the game. Remember, your paradigms and fears show up when you are in action. When that happens, remember the tools in this Key. Then, highlight or write them down as a reminder to yourself. Because the paradigms that create our fear stories are tricky, they can make us forget how to listen to that part of us that wants to move forward and claim our victory.

Suzanne Durnan, the CEO at Simplified Financial in Maple Ridge, B.C., is one of my clients in the VIP Mastermind Group. She cares deeply for her clients and is diligent in educating them so they are empowered to make the best decisions for themselves. Her team is well known for going above and beyond; they ensure that every client and their families and businesses are protected, and their investments grow.

However, Suzanne was harboring a hidden block that was holding her back: the fear of outshining. She did not grow up in a prosperous family and had a story running in her mind of what people would think if she was too successful. She said, "I never want anyone to assume I think I am better than anyone else."

A common hidden barrier to success for women is the fear of being disloyal or leaving friends and family behind. We tend to pull back from striving for success if we fear we'll end up alone or worry about abandoning our roots and leaving the people we love behind. Her paradigm showed up as fear of losing the clients she loves.

Through the personal growth experienced in the VIP Mastermind Group, she gained more confidence, getting in touch with the specialized service she brings to her clients by treating them like family. Suzanne says, "My commitment is treating every client like the unique individual they are, with their particular circumstances." As her confidence in herself grew, her fear of success diminished. As a result, her business increased 30% this year, capitulating her already successful enterprise closer to the million-dollar range.

Remember what happened to me when I was in the Bahamas? It does not matter how aware we have become or how long we have been in the world of personal growth, our paradigms still show up, and the key is to use the tools we have to interrupt them to maintain self-mastery.

The key is that your vision must be bigger than your fear! You will never be afraid in your comfort zone. So, when fear appears, you know you are moving beyond your comfort zone, limitations, and boundaries into the realm where your dreams live.

"Do one thing every day that scares you."
—Eleanor Roosevelt

Key #7
Break Through Invisible Barriers

I broke through my limitations and released myself from the chains of my story. Now it's time for you to soar into the clear blue skies of *your* boundless dreams!

Encoded in Key #7 is the secret to breaking free of your glass ceiling. Declaring a dream, goal, or vision does not guarantee it will become a reality. Writing it out, visualizing it, and intensely wanting what we want is not enough in and of itself to bring it into being. Our inner beliefs must be aligned with our vision.

Now that you have fully permitted yourself to dream of a life you would love, it's time to become aware of the limiting beliefs that, if left unchecked, become ingrained patterns that block you. Together, we'll shine a light on how to become conscious of those invisible patterns so you can break through the barriers that hold you back or stop you from living your dream life.

As you read on, consider where you are now, where you want to be, and what lies hidden in the gap. If you find yourself in never-ending situations that you do not want, let's dive deeper and find out why that is; and more importantly, what to do about it. Take some time and really lean into these exercises I am about to share. The awareness you can gain from them is life-changing. I intend to present these awareness exercises as simply as possible, with as much depth as necessary for you to have everything you require to break through anything that is in the way of your success.

Some of this material may feel repetitive—I hope you notice if it does. That means you are becoming more aware of what gets in the way of all that you sense is possible yet cannot materialize. Repetition is a significant ingredient for transformation. So come back to this Key again and again, and let it be the key that helps free you from any cage in which you feel locked.

The universal pull to growth and freedom is infinitely more powerful than our patterns and paradigms.

So how do we recognize and release patterns of thinking or behaviors that are not in harmony with the image of the life we want to live?

Working with mentors who have more understanding than I have made the most significant difference for me. For this reason, I say, "Let's do this together." We can all rise and fulfill the calling of our souls when we are supported and work together. Our level of awareness creates our results.

We all have blind spots, and just as I could not identify my inner blocks on my own, I believe that no one can see what is holding them back without some help. Even when I did start to see them, I did not know how to change them. I needed both awareness and tools to stop repeating the patterns that kept me stuck and wanting to give up.

Einstein said, "We can't solve problems by using the same kind of thinking we used when we created them."

It's a bit of a Catch-22 when you sense bigger possibilities for yourself while harboring a core belief that does not align with that *knowing*. If a part of you is stuck in an old, powerless story, it causes an internal struggle, and you may feel conflicted or resistant to what you sense is possible.

We all have a predominant operating system or set of beliefs by which we live our lives. These patterns set the amount of abundance we allow into our lives. It shows up in our money, love, relationships, happiness, health, and essentially all the areas that are important to us.

I distinctly remember the first time I discovered the depth of embedded behavioral patterns that either serve us or sabotage us in creating the results we want in our lives.

I was studying to become a yoga teacher and was reading a book by B.K.S. Iyengar when I had a profound awakening. I experienced a surge of awareness and, for the first time in my life, I saw why I could not get the results I wanted and, no matter how hard I tried, would only get so far and could not go beyond my inner glass ceiling.

In *Light on Life,* Iyengar said,

> In order to have freedom, we must understand how our ingrained habits and patterns of behavior or conditioned reflexes so often control us. Since ingrained patterns of behavior, which yoga calls samskara or subliminal impressions, lie, as the word subliminal suggests, largely in our unconscious, it is in our own interest to emphasize the new and positive action and not dwell on the negative past.

Iyengar teaches that yoga is a powerful tool for liberating ourselves from unwanted, ingrained patterns, which I've found to be true in my years of practicing yoga. Discovering unconscious patterns was life-changing, and I have since studied this philosophy with many personal growth masters.

Limiting beliefs are developed at a young age. Whenever something negative happened, we gave meaning to that experience. We interpreted every negative comment said to us, every disappointment, rejection, or hurt, and turned them into a story about ourselves, other people, or the world around us. And we believed that story.

That story you told yourself stayed with you over the years. It made you see the world through a particular lens; that lens you've been looking through has created your results today.

Most of us have limiting perceptions of ourselves that create a sense of doubt about the possibilities for our life. We beg the question, "I am an intelligent woman, so why is this still happening to me?" Please do not blame yourself. It happens to all of us because, as I stated earlier, limiting beliefs and paradigms are sneaky and deceptive. Fortunately, it is possible to bring them to consciousness, repattern them, and walk a path of success.

Past research suggests females are more likely to blame themselves, believing they are flawed when shamed, punished, or getting into trouble for something. By contrast, males are more likely to externalize their feelings, directing them outward. My stories, and those of many women I've worked with over the years, go very deep. Our stories tell us who we are and what is or is not possible for us. Up until now!

Consider how elephants are trained in some countries. As an infant, one leg is bound by a rope tied to a stake in the ground. At this stage of development, they cannot break free from the rope around their leg. It is painful if they try, and eventually, they give up. Later in life, when fully grown, they could break free but don't. They have been conditioned to believe more in the power of the constraint than in their own strength. Unaware of their capacity to set themselves free, they end up as mature elephants still tied to a stake.

We can all break free of the conditions in our life that are not in alignment with our dreams. What it requires is becoming aware of our true power and taking action. Humans have the capacity to become more consciously aware, whereas animals do not. They cannot change how they were trained or conditioned and, as such, often accept it as their reality.

It is imperative to develop an acute awareness of the thoughts and beliefs that are not aligned with our dream life, so we can interrupt the stories running under the surface that hinder our capacity to excel. I am not referring to random thoughts. But instead, the repeated dominating thoughts running on a well-worn path in our mind, which cause the automatic patterns of how we feel, act and react, and create the outcomes we experience.

Our higher self—the infinite side of us—longs for the life we would love. Meanwhile, our human side pulls us back to the familiar, whether we like being there or not.

This seventh key is pivotal to manifesting your dream life. It is time to identify and release what has been shaping your life and keeping you stuck.

I love this quote by my mentor, Mary Morrissey: "Our awareness of our patterns is the first step toward designing the life for which we were intended."

To break through to the next level of success, you must identify the pattern of stuckness or limitation in the area with which you are most dissatisfied.

You identified that area of discontent in Key #1 while doing the life assessment exercise. Although, if that area is causing you pain in such a way that it is on your mind constantly, you may not need to look back. There can be a lot of emotional energy in the areas where we feel blocked.

The thoughts and energy of non-possibility can leave you feeling hopeless and powerless. Like the baby elephant, it can be crippling when we believe our limitations are the truth. In my own experience, it can be painful looking at the places where we are getting stuck or stopped. So be gentle with yourself. No self-judgment is allowed.

To tap back into the power within you, you must disrupt the pattern to break the invisible chains of bondage. I will share a powerful exercise I created called, Tapping into Your True Power. However, before I do that, I would like to share a breakthrough from one of my clients who diligently practiced this exercise.

Brenda had been feeling stuck in the area of Time & Money Freedom for over twenty-five years. No matter what she did, she continued to reach a maximum limit of $150,000 in her business, year after year, some years as low as $120,000. The result she wanted for all those years was to double her income with ease, yet what she felt was a tremendous amount of resistance.

When we got curious about the resistance and she started noticing her thoughts, we discovered something about her pattern. We saw that she had some opposing beliefs that created a glass ceiling keeping her stuck at that income level no matter how hard she worked.

She noticed that she believed working harder was the *only* way to create more money. So, she would work more and push harder for increased results.

At one point, she came up with the idea that she would take on a second client whose services were compatible with the product her current corporate client offered. Lo and behold, she landed the ideal client. The only mandate both clients had was that she produce the sales results they wanted, which was entirely possible with the structure she had in place. However, she vividly recalls her thoughts turning negative after the initial excitement wore off.

Brenda's negative thought pattern of "working too hard" kicked in. When she did not interrupt that pattern, she began telling herself the story that both companies would expect her to work what equated to the hours of two full-time jobs. More than expecting it, she believed they would also get mad if she did not work harder, which tapped into her anger about others controlling her. This familiar feeling caused her to become resistant to going forward. It was like she had one foot on the gas, ready to break through her glass ceiling, and the other on the brakes, afraid of being controlled.

She was thinking about the job non-stop from the minute her eyes opened until she went to sleep; sometimes, even waking in the middle of the night with it on her mind. In the end, she kept trying harder, working more, having no fun, feeling tense and uptight, and not producing the desired results for herself or her clients.

What Brenda realized is that she made her lack of results mean that she was doing something wrong, and she must need someone else to tell her how to do the job *right*. But at the same time, she also resisted being told what to do. That entire scenario left her feeling what she calls "jammed up," which she calls feeling under pressure and powerless.

The truth for Brenda as a saleswoman is that her gift is selling with heart and integrity. She is committed to offering only products and services that create success for her clients. When she was stuck in her old pattern and story, rather than working from her gift, it became a glass ceiling for her that kept the pressure on and a lid on her abundance.

Once she identified her limiting patterns and disrupted her negative thoughts by working more closely with me, she tapped into that power that lives in all of us and focused on the truth that we live in an abundant universe. That is when the penny dropped—in the form of doubling her income.

She also discovered that as she let go of her negative thinking and repatterned her beliefs, she opened herself to other avenues of abundance that required little or no effort on her part. In shifting the "log jam" that existed in her old patterns and beliefs, the trickle of abundance became a huge flow.

I am so thrilled that Brenda gave me permission to share her struggle with you to encourage you to see what might be holding you back from creating whatever you would love to manifest at the next level. There is more to Brenda's story. However, can you see how the story takes on a life of its own—one that may be relatable to many of us? Most of us have a variation of a similar pattern that we are not aware of that keeps us stuck and shut down to possibilities.

As I do with all my clients, I shared with Brenda the underlying principle in creating our dreams:

The point of power is within, and what is within us is far greater than anything in our surroundings.

When we are in harmony with our soul's purpose, in alignment with who we are here to be and what we are here to do, things get easier, and anything is possible. However, when we listen to and believe those old stories, they become patterns that are the invisible inner barrier to our success.

Brenda broke through that invisible barrier. As a result, she has substantially increased her wealth. All while being more relaxed and having more fun than she has ever had.

So exciting, isn't it? Many years ago, I discovered the only way I could empower myself to create a new result was to look inside, as Brenda did, at my thoughts and beliefs. My pilgrimage has shifted me from the fixed mindset that life was happening *to* me by something outside my control to the understanding that I am a co-creator with life.

I discovered that I had the power to change everything I felt was happening to me. Keeping my old stories and tapes running in my mind held my patterns of failure in place. What an eye-opener! When I first realized what was happening, I was discouraged and more than a little resistant to that idea. Yet, once I started breaking through the familiar resistance, it was the MOST empowering discovery I have ever made.

The entire journey to find my freedom was inward; that is where it is for all of us. Life is constantly responding to our inner stories.

Are you ready for the quest?

Pattern Awareness Process
Tapping into your true power

As you do this exercise, know that we all have a part of us that is wise and all-knowing, that wise woman in us that is spiritual in nature, the part we might call our soul or inner goddess. It is where our wisdom and intuition dwell.

Begin with this centering practice: Find a quiet place where you will not be interrupted for about thirty minutes. If it feels right for you, put on some quiet, reflective music. Take a posture of empowerment with your back straight and your upper chest.

Bring your awareness to your body, starting at the soles of your feet, connected to the earth, and imagine roots coming from the bottom of your feet extending into the earth and bringing the rich nutrients of the earth back up into your body to rejuvenate you. Feel it moving up your ankles, knees, thighs, and hips. This beautiful rich earth energy, life-giving prana, continues moving up your body into your solar plexus, spine, and heart chakra, gracefully across your shoulders, down your arms, and into the tips of your fingers.

Continue to breathe slowly and deeply as this relaxing energy moves up your neck into your face, your jaw, and then up and out the top of your head. Notice how much more relaxed you are feeling.

From this relaxed and tranquil state, picture a moment or an experience in your life where you felt loved. Imagine it happening right now in the present. It might be when you were with a beloved pet, or a time with your child, your best friend, or maybe a grandparent. Allow the full expression of love to expand your heart.

Now, picture yourself when you are showing up as that same expression of love and caring. What do you notice? See yourself in a moment of feeling and expressing kindness, love, and wisdom. Connect with yourself as you take a deep breath in through your nose and exhale through your mouth. If you find it helpful, tune into your deepest inner self by tapping gently with your middle and index finger on the top of your head for about ten seconds. In EFT/Tapping, this action is what I call *tuning in*.

From this loving, centered place within yourself, this connected, deeper source of love—your highest self—say the following affirmation out loud, "I utilize this love to be free and to break through to the next best version of me."

Bring to mind the four major areas of your life: Health & Well-Being, Love & Relationships (including your relationship with yourself and your spirituality), Vocation (your creative expression), and Time & Money Freedom.

Think about something in one of those areas that you are not completely happy with, where you feel stuck or cannot get the desired result. Become curious. Does this feel familiar to you? Has it happened before? Are you still getting the same results that keep you from getting any closer to the life you long to live, no matter what you do?

It can be confronting and vulnerable to look at our history. As you go into this reflection, I want to reassure you there is no blame or shame in this process. If it helps, take on the role of detective, looking for clues to identify any patterns that may be blocking your success.

Take time to identify a struggle or frustration. For example:

- Another relationship you thought was "the one," is not the one, after all.
- You lose the weight only to regain it.
- You work hard yet are always in debt or cannot seem to get ahead.
- You finally get some money put away, then something breaks down, or another unexpected expense occurs.
- You get the new perfect job, yet you end up as unhappy as you were in the last one.
- You promise to keep your home organized, and it is, for a short time. Then before you know it, disorganization has taken over.

- You decide to make a change in the morning, and by the end of the day, you're back to the same old habit.

Now that you have brought to mind an area of your life that you feel is challenging you, pick up your journal and write whatever comes to you at this moment. Write down any insights or memories that you recall.

I know it may not be comfortable to do this; however, get very specific about the last time this unwanted result happened. Or precisely what is happening now, if the struggle is current.

We often want to blame something or someone outside of ourselves, leaving us feeling like victims. You will gain the greatest awareness by looking first at your thoughts in these situations, then at the story you spun from those thoughts— where it all starts. The easiest way to know what you were thinking is to look at your results. Results do not lie.

With that in mind, I have given you nine questions for reflection to assist you in gaining awareness. I also include an example of what one of my clients discovered during this revealing exercise.

Take your time and remember to keep breathing while you do this writing exercise. Our patterns have a life force of their own. Although they may start with our thoughts, they live in our bodies, not our minds.

1. What are my thoughts about this condition or situation that keeps happening?

2. What emotion am I feeling, and where do I feel it in my body? Place your hand there and see if

you can identify any specific characteristics of the emotion, maybe a color, a shape, or a weight.

3. What is the story I am telling myself about why this situation is happening? Who is to blame, me or someone else?

4. When I tell this story, or worry about not getting what I want, what is my reaction, action, or lack of action? How does it negatively affect me?

5. What do the behaviors of this pattern lead to?

6. How long do I stay in this state?

7. How much of my energy does it consume, and how much focus does it take?

8. What belief have I formed about myself in this area I have identified?

9. What is the cost of not transforming this limiting story and pattern?

Your pattern has a life force. The minute you say, with conviction, **"I AM DONE WITH THIS!"** it gets given *notice* that it cannot run the show anymore. YOU are in control!

Let me give you an example from a client of mine, Dawnalee. She is a smart, single, vivacious, fun-loving, middle-aged woman; these are her reflections on the pattern awareness exercise.

"The result I want is a committed relationship with a life partner who is also my best friend. Yet, I cannot seem to create this. The romances I have are casual and fun, but never form into anything real. I tend to choose men who are not interested in or able to have a serious relationship, and am rarely attracted to ones who do seem to want something deeper with me."

1. Thoughts: I don't get it. I used to be in demand. Did I lose my spark? Is it me or the guys I choose? It's not just one guy; it seems to be every guy I've dated since I left my husband. So, what about me isn't good enough to want as a partner? Is there something wrong with me? I still think I'm an amazing catch; however, I get stuck on this belief that I am intrinsically flawed in some ways that might deter a potential partner.

2. Emotions: I feel frustrated, hopeless, deeply sad, and angry. And I'm becoming cynical. I notice these feelings showing up in my heart, solar plexus, and shoulders.

3. Story I am telling myself: I am not enough. I'm not the kind of woman guys want to marry. I'm appealing and desirable but more of a novelty, like test-driving an exotic car with no real interest in buying it. Or a toy to enjoy in secret, whenever they feel like it, but not enough to have proudly in their lives, without reservation. I am somehow different and always have been, never fitting into the norm. I'm not treated with respect, and I blame both the men I allow into my life and myself for tolerating it.

4. How this story affects me negatively: I feel like I'm not good enough, that I'm deeply flawed and not worth their effort. I feel discardable. It makes me think men are selfish and heartless, and I

react with shame and anger, which shuts down my heart and makes me want to give up and *just not bother* trying.

5. Behaviors this story leads to: I check out from the world, hide at home alone, refuse to answer the phone or engage with people, and overeat junk food while binge-watching shows. Or, refusing to be a victim and let "them" win, I go the opposite route and respond with an old rebellious behavior, overextending myself socially, over-indulging, and making decisions that don't honor my highest self or align with the vision of what I *truly* want. This defiance has led to dating guys who offer less than what I'm looking for, and I play casual in an attempt to stay in control, not get attached, and avoid the risk of being hurt or rejected.

6. How long do I stay in this state: I can stay in either extreme for many days, often until I have to go to work or am forced to face some other unavoidable responsibility.

7. How much energy does it take: It completely zaps my energy, mentally and physically, and drains me to the point where I'm too exhausted to do anything. And I end up lying around feeling depressed, too unmotivated to care.

8. The belief I have formed about myself: I am not worthy or lovable. I don't fit it in or belong. I am broken, and very likely to end up alone.

9. The cost of not transforming this: I will end up alone, bitter, and a little crazy. I will never have a partner in life or the love I deeply desire.

When doing this exercise, Dawnalee realized she was playing out an old story that stemmed from beliefs formed in childhood and perpetuated throughout her adult life. While working with me to reclaim her power, she made the decision to stop being a woman who accepts breadcrumbs—from anyone—and is now a self-love diva, acknowledging and honoring herself as a goddess.

Through her dedicated work in DreamBuilders, she has repatterned her old paradigms that, up until now, have blocked love. She learned to say NO to men who offer anything less than her heart's desire and YES to being treated the way she *knows* she deserves: with love, adoration, respect, and honor! Having broken free from the past, Dawnalee is now creating positive experiences and a powerful new story.

The future you are stepping into necessitates some letting go, calls for some healing—not because you are broken, but because you are on this human journey—and requires you to begin something new. Once you gain awareness, you can rewrite your story. Your life's journey unfolds into the story you tell yourself and, when focused on, becomes your reality.

Have you done this exercise for yourself? If so, let's move immediately into repatterning it so you can lift yourself to higher ground. Here is how!

This is a *very* important step, and I spend concentrated time with the women I coach to begin the transformation process on their way to freedom.

It is time to repattern this story and these beliefs. Whatever you do, do NOT skip over this part and stay stuck in the thoughts and feelings of what you uncovered for yourself.

Begin by breathing in deeply. Now stand up and shake it off. Lift your arms above your head and shake it all off. Then shake each leg. Shake until you start to feel lighter. If you are so inclined, move your whole body. Stretch, dance, clap, whatever shifts your energy in this moment. If you have any music that speaks to your heart, put it on, turn up the volume, and move your body!

Ahhhh! Way to go! Now, let's repattern.

We all have a way of temporarily escaping our patterned thoughts and behaviors that cause us pain. For example, we may get instant gratification from random shopping, overeating, or other addictive behaviors. Even healthy habits such as journalling or going for a run, talking to our friends, or doing yoga may not be enough in and of themselves to break free of the unconscious limiting beliefs that cause results you do not want.

Would you love to permanently repattern and transform this stuck area into a positive, empowering pattern of results you love? This next step is how you do that.

Tap into your higher self—Wise Woman, Goddess, Queen—who you are, that powerful part of you. We all have her; however, we do not always access that part of ourselves, especially when the patterns in the way of our greatness have been in place for a long time. Do not be disheartened if this seems true for you.

If you are feeling challenged at this moment to tap into that sage part of you, I invite you to think of someone you helped or in whose life you made a difference, and how that made you feel. Another powerful method is to think of some of your greatest successes.

Close your eyes and visualize yourself in the roles and situations where you were WINNING, where YOU ROCKED IT and felt POWERFUL!

Maxwell Maltz, in *The Magic Power of Self-Image Psychology,* says: "I can foresee victories for the person who gets that winning feeling, that image of him/herself in successful roles." This exercise helps raise your self-esteem.

He goes on to say that an image of winning carries a big punch. Keep picturing yourself in your successes over and over until you can *feel* yourself in your BEST moments.

From this place inside yourself, rewrite your pattern into a new story or vision. Set your to-do list aside, light a candle, and take your time to be still.

An effective writing prompt to help inspire the creative process is: "Once upon a time, I received the miracle of a re-birth. I was blessed with the opportunity to awaken into the magnificence of who I am. And today, what is most important to me and what matters most is..."

If you want to learn how to rewrite the painful stories of your past and live freely, this prompt and many others are offered in the Re-Write Your Life Program created by Junie Swadron.

Now, craft a Loving, Empowering Truth Statement out of the writing exercise, such as the following examples.

- I am loved in every relationship; I am loved, and I am enough.
- I am deeply loved and valued as a child of the Universe.

- I honor my desires and needs, and my well-being is my number one priority.
- The more I value myself, the easier my dreams manifest.
- I am completely open to love, support, and success at every level.
- I am blessed.
- I AM ENOUGH. I always have enough time, enough money, enough love, and enough support to live a life I absolutely love.

As I opened myself to more of what I would love, I created the acronym **L.E.T.S.**—**L**oving, **E**mpowering, **T**ruth, **S**tatement. When you have crafted your statement or statements, read them every single day. Put them in places where you will see them often. I write mine on sticky notes and paste them all over my office, where I spend a lot of time. Use **L.E.T.S.** like a mantra to **L**ove yourself, **E**mpower yourself, and be the **T**ruth of you that propels you to **S**oar!

My power decree helps me bridge the gap between where I am and where I want to be. So, L.E.T.S. do this!

Another tool for repatterning our limiting beliefs is this process I teach from the DreamBuilder Program:

Step 1. Notice and identify a limiting belief.

Step 2. Take a deep, comfortable breath in through your nose, then purse your lips and breathe out of your mouth like you are blowing out of a straw. Repeat three times.

Step 3. Decide on the new belief you want, then create a statement starting with the words, ***"Up until now,*** *I thought* (whatever your limiting thought was), ***and now I believe***

(insert your new belief)." Repeat this declaration for thirty days and say it every time you notice that limiting belief.

These are powerful tools to aid you in transforming limiting beliefs. But it wouldn't be fair if I did not tell you that these patterns are deep, strong, and layered. So be diligent with yourself and consider a system of support.

We do not always change voluntarily. Habits are stubborn. Many times, we must experience pain, which then becomes the motivation for real transformation. In my introduction, I gave you the quote by Michael Beckwith that says, "Pain pushes us until a larger vision pulls us."

Change happens fastest in one of two ways. One is with a proven structure of support that provides the space, time, and repetition to help you install your NEW empowering beliefs on a subconscious level (aka: installing a new set point for your success.)

If you do not love the results in every area of your life, get yourself into a structure of support, whether it's a teacher, mentor, or coach who has accomplished the results you deeply desire. If being supported calls to you and you have no one in your life to offer that now, reach out and contact me through my website www. patriciacampbell.ca and I promise I will invite you to the next workshop I hold. I make that promise because I know first-hand that the second way to create change is with a strong emotional impact. Unfortunately, many people wait and do not find a structured support system, and therefore do not change until they experience a significant *wake-up call.* Although, there are positive events that can be a paradigm shifter as well, like having a baby or getting married.

When you first hear the whispers of your soul trying to get your attention, listen closely and find a mastermind group that is growth oriented. We cannot break free in isolation. An entire chapter of *Think and Grow Rich* is devoted to the power of a properly chosen Mastermind group for the definite purpose of creating higher results. When writing about the Mastermind Principle, Napoleon Hill says, "Great power can be accumulated through no other principle."

We cannot become ourselves by ourselves.

Key #8
The Power of Love

You have declared the results you would love and designed a vision that you are passionate about that has you feeling blissful. By tapping into the power of love, you can make the quantum leap to manifesting the sacred vision that is the blueprint of your life.

Creating a life you love requires your thoughts and feelings to be in sync with the desired results. What—and how—we think is critical, as thought becomes form. As we learned in The Results Formula, all thoughts carry a creative force.

Investing the time and effort to consistently self-reflect and identify where we are progressing and where there is still work to do is a primary factor in what we manifest.

In my rigorous study with Brave Thinking Institute to become a life and business coach, I finally began understanding how the Universal Laws work. Many of us have heard of the Law of Attraction. I teach principles using this law in one of my coaching programs. However, I have learned that it is secondary to the Law of Vibration.

In *Power vs. Force,* Dr. David R. Hawkins offers The Map of Consciousness, a proven energy scale to actualize your ultimate potential. He used a unique muscle-testing method, conducting over 250,000 calibrations during twenty years of research to define a range of values, attitudes, and emotions that correspond to levels of consciousness. This range of values—along with a logarithmic scale of one to one thousand—became The Map of Consciousness.

In The Map, Dr. Hawkins lays out the entire spectrum of consciousness from lower levels, such as Shame and Guilt, up to Courage and Willingness, and then to more expanded levels of Love, Peace, and Enlightenment. He gives the energy level of each emotion and claims these higher frequencies are carrier waves of immense life force.

Using Dr. Hawkins' work to our advantage requires us to become aware of raising our vibration to a higher level through our thoughts and actions. Einstein said it this way, "Everything is energy. That's all there is. Match the frequency of the reality you want, and it cannot help but be yours. This is not philosophy, it is physics."

The key, then, is to hold a frequency that aligns with what we want to create in our lives. When we maintain that frequency—the vibration that matches what we would love—our lives begin to reflect that in reality. Put simply, when we raise our vibration to the higher states, we become a match with the results we desire.

If we have a pattern of thinking and speaking negatively, it slows down or blocks our success. If we only think unloving, critical thoughts about ourselves, we create a feeling in our body of not being loved, which in turn causes a vibration lower than love. Do you suppose we can easily manifest a loving relationship while feeling negative about ourselves and, therefore, unworthy of being loved?

In *Dynamic Laws of Prosperity,* Catherine Ponder says, "If you criticize your world, you repel its blessings and attract only negative, limited conditions into your life."

We create what we put out into the world. For example, if I am looking to attract my soulmate or want more love in my life, yet I am criticizing myself, I am projecting the message that I am not lovable; therefore, I am not a match with the love I crave.

This principle is true whether you are single and wanting to attract the love of your life or you have a life partner and are craving more love in your relationship. One of the passageways to creating love in your life is to begin loving yourself. Falling madly in love with yourself, grateful and proud every day of who you are and what you are creating in your life, is the ultimate way to ensure the best results. Even a little more self-love than you currently have begins to open the portal. Become best friends with yourself. How do you treat your best friend? Do you speak differently to her than you do to yourself?

If you want to play a bigger game and live a life of abundance but have even an iota of low self-esteem, I urge you to begin a practice of self-love right away. Make this *non-negotiable.* You, loving you! What a concept to consider! I believe it is the most important practice you can offer yourself. Why? Because without loving yourself, or at the very least liking and accepting yourself exactly as you are, wherever you are, you cannot grow in the ways you anticipate.

For this very reason, relationships have been the most challenging aspect of my whole, entire life. A few years ago, when I was still not feeling loved wholeheartedly, I realized *my* heart was not full of love. After all the years and effort I had put into creating the life of my dreams, the love I longed for was still not mine. Things had improved significantly; however, something was still missing.

It felt like there was still a gaping hole inside me, starving for love and affection. I carried a lot of negative feelings about myself and my relationships. Yet, I tried too hard and stayed too long in relationships where I did not feel loved or honored—both personally and in work situations. I thought if I fought hard enough, things would eventually change. I was looking for love, acceptance, and approval from outside sources instead of generating it from inside myself.

I noticed I continued to recreate those experiences, not realizing I had the power to change any of it. At that time, I was unaware, but I now see it was a pattern in my life. Did I miss the secret of the ages—that me loving myself was the most powerful key of all? What I did have going for me was determination. I was tenaciously committed to finding happiness, peace, and deep love. So much so that I seldom appreciated the great things I already had in my life because I was so focused on what I felt was lacking.

I had a story, and I kept telling it. Little did I know, the more I told my sad tale, the more I perpetuated it. I felt trapped, stuck in the vortex, and could not get out no matter how hard I tried. I wanted to be loved in the ways I felt I needed to be, which was different from how my husband and others showed me their love. Unfortunately, I unknowingly blocked the love available to me because I failed to recognize how they expressed love.

That is the insidiousness of our patterns. They can be in control for our entire lives and, if left untransformed, lead us astray and deprive us of our birthright of happiness. However, when we are happy and loving ourselves and our lives, we radiate a high vibration that magnetizes more of what we love. Like attracts like. Love attracts love!

Have you ever spent time around someone excited by their life? The energy they exude is exhilarating, and you feel enlivened in their presence. *This* energy is a significant factor in attracting more love into your life. A perfect example is how I was feeling when I met my husband, Colin. I was working as a volunteer, creating workshops for teenage girls to increase their self-esteem. I loved this fulfilling work and felt like I was on top of the world.

The Law of Attraction breaks down to this: You attract what you give energy to. Therefore, you must expect the result you would love to have; otherwise, it is just wishing or hoping it happens. In creating what I would love, I focus on the end result. For example, I visualize the workshops I lead. I see myself celebrating the breakthroughs of the women I coach. I picture myself having fun with my family. I coach all the women in the DreamBuilder Program to picture themselves in scenes they love—ones that vividly show them they have fulfilled the vision in their hearts.

By now, you have likely figured out I love knowing how to accomplish my heart's desire. In my experience, *gratitude* and *forgiveness* are the two most powerful tools to raise our vibration and change results.

Gratitude positively affects your vibrational frequency. I can personally attest to this reality. There was a time in my life when I saw what was wrong far more than what was right; like looking at a house covered in beautiful Christmas lights and focusing on the one that was burned out. It came to my attention that I had a generally negative attitude. For something as simple as a burned-out light, it may not matter, but when I was so focused on everything less-than-awesome, I couldn't appreciate all the things that were incredible.

Throughout this book, you've likely noticed a theme that illustrates I was a very unhappy woman; I thought I had a right to be that way. I was righteously indignant! I truly felt I could not make my life work, at least not how I wanted it to. It seemed to me it was hit or miss, and I desperately wanted a change.

Gratitude is one of the fastest and easiest ways to amp up our vibration and create change. Try it right now. Stop reading for a moment and bring to mind one thing for which you are grateful. Take a deep breath, and as you exhale, just feel or sense that one thing. Pause and call to mind a person, event, or experience you are thankful for, and notice if it evokes any deeper feelings or emotions that feel good to you.

I had a transformational experience when I was living in Australia. As I described earlier, when I remarried and moved across the world to be with my husband, all I could think about was returning home to Canada, where my children and grandchildren lived. But unfortunately, that was not happening as quickly as I wanted, and I often felt frustrated. In addition to my fabulous grandson, Traimin, who was born in Canada while I was in Australia, my phenomenal granddaughter, Taryn, was born two years later, so my yearning to get "home" intensified.

I realized I had become quite critical of myself, my husband, life in Australia, and the world in general. I cannot remember exactly how I learned about the gratitude practice I tried out of desperation. However, I do remember reading that what you focus on expands, so it seemed a wise move to look at something that could make me happy.

I bought myself a beautiful little notebook, which became my gratitude journal, and committed to writing five things for which I was grateful every day. I started to notice the little things I took for granted, like a comfortable bed, my warm jacket on a cold day, the abundance of food in the fridge, and hot water for a shower. I was shocked at how fast it affected my feelings and attitude.

As I wrote what I was grateful for, the more I was aware of the abundance in my life instead of the lack. I became less critical of my husband because I began to notice and remember the qualities that I admired in him. The more I did this mindful appreciation, the more fun we had together, the happier I felt, and the more harmonious my marriage became.

I also began to appreciate the stunning land of Australia. I fell in love with the beauty of the country I was blessed to live in for that short time. I took up the practice of running on the sandy beaches of the spectacular Indian Ocean and witnessed the dolphins jumping high in the air as if to increase my new feelings of joy.

Gratitude is now a regular practice for me and has been instrumental in accessing more abundance in love, wealth, and good health. Gratitude opens our hearts and increases the love in us. That has been my experience, and I invite you to get curious and try it as a regular practice. The best way to accept whether something is right for you is to try it out and see what happens.

One of my favorite quotes from Rumi is,

> Be grateful for your life, every detail of it, and your face will come to shine like a sun, and everyone who sees it will be made glad and peaceful. Persist in gratitude, and you will slowly become one with the Sun of Love, and Love will shine through you its all-healing joy.

Here is an exercise to increase your gratitude and elevate your vibration to a higher level.

Gratitude Practice

1. Set an intention for a result you would love in your life.

2. For the next thirty days, write three to five things you are grateful for. It is best to do this practice first thing in the morning, before the busyness of your day starts, or as the last thing before you go to sleep.

3. Begin to notice if your day is any different than it usually is, and keep a journal noting what you become aware of. No matter how small or insignificant you think it might be, record it so you have evidence of how many instances you experience.

Albert Einstein said, "There are only two ways to live your life. One, as though nothing is a miracle, and the other as though everything is a miracle."

A woman who knows the power of gratitude and has produced miracles in her life is one of my clients, Gaetane. When I met her, she was searching for answers to questions like: Who am I? How do I create my dreams? Is there more to life than just work and retirement?

Gaetane plays full out and puts her heart into the gratitude practice we begin every session with, never wavering from starting her day giving thanks. Gratitude is on the frequency of abundance, and she is a testament to what is possible when you live in a state of gratitude. The wins she celebrates are plentiful, but her greatest victory is learning to look inward to find her answers and, in doing so, discovering her soul's passion and purpose. Gaetane is a woman who shines her light brightly!

Sometimes before we can get to that state, we have some forgiveness work to do. The doorway to fully opening my heart was learning how to forgive those I felt betrayed or hurt me. That was my beginning. I now realize that not everyone has the capacity to love fully and unconditionally.

I can choose to have anger or compassion for those people in my life who cannot love wholeheartedly. I primarily choose compassion, although it sometimes takes me a while. When I do not, I am fully aware and choose again because I know there is a cost to not forgiving. So, I set an intention to forgive myself for my anger and find compassion for both that person and me.

How do we take the actual steps toward forgiveness? I believe forgiveness is a process, not a one-time event.

Even when we consciously decide to forgive someone, resentment may creep back in. It takes some diligence and rigor.

While forgiveness does not change our past, it changes the way we think about the people or situations we are forgiving, which, in turn, brings peace to the life we are living now.

I believe you can heal your heart through forgiveness, and a pivotal component of forgiveness is moving away from victimhood. First, I had to stop blaming my unhappiness on anyone else.

Not forgiving others leads to bitterness and, similarly, to self-contempt when we don't forgive ourselves. It gnaws away at you. My experience told me, with no uncertainty, that regardless of whether resentment, anger, or bitterness is projected out toward others or stuffed inward, it is destructive to the soul.

Remember that forgiveness does not give license to people to treat us as they please, nor does it mean that those who have hurt or abused us get to be part of our lives. We are doing our inner work for ourselves, not for them.

Forgiveness is a major element in setting ourselves free, allowing more positivity into our lives so we can direct energy into successfully building our dreams.

A lack of forgiveness is a stumbling block in the gap between where we are right now and the vision we hold for the life we would love. Lack of forgiveness may show up as holding onto feelings of blame, resentment, anger, or betrayal.

Every woman I have ever worked with has experienced betrayal. It could have been someone close to us, perhaps a job, an institution, or maybe we felt our body let us down. We get to decide whether we will allow that experience to make us bitter or make us better.

Some questions to ask yourself are: Is there a hurt I'm still carrying? How can I rewrite that story in a way that is empowering? How can I turn that experience into something that makes me feel better? I often ask myself these questions when practicing forgiveness. I cannot say I have to look far, especially for the hurts and betrayals that cut the deepest.

Then I read this quote by Catherine Ponder, "When you hold resentment toward another, you are bound to that person or condition by an emotional link that is stronger than steel. Forgiveness is the only way to dissolve that link and get free."

That woke me up! I became serious about forgiving anyone and everyone toward whom I have ever held any resentment. Since that awareness, I continue to actively practice forgiveness. And I will tell you there are times I have to do it daily, especially when something triggers pain or anger in me. When that happens, my mind (my ego) jumps in with the old story of why I should stay angry, annoyed, or sometimes downright outraged.

If we judge ourselves for what we think we have done wrong and have created a story of who we are because of that, then we often shrink, play small, or hide. Those are contractive vibrations. To birth our dreams, it is essential for us to be in an expansive vibration of love. There is always a cost to staying in the resonance of shame, guilt, or regret.

I had no idea how much self-loathing I had for the mistakes I had made in my life until I started to pay attention to my inner critic. I criticized myself mercilessly, especially when I felt I had failed as a mother. Until I learned to practice self- forgiveness, I was unknowingly withholding love from myself.

When we withhold love from ourselves, we also keep out the love of others and the abundance of life that would naturally come to us in all the ways that abundance can show up.

Forgiving myself set me free. I did this by using mirror exercises and the forgiveness practice of Ho'oponopono. Many books and other resources talk about the healing power of this Hawaiian forgiveness process. I started by looking in the mirror every day for thirty days, saying my name out loud while looking directly into my eyes. Next, I said three to five things I was proud of or liked about myself. And finally, three to five things I wanted to forgive myself for. Then, when I thought of those incidents, I said the Ho'oponopono prayer, the way I understand it: "I am sorry. Please forgive me. Thank You. I love you."

Dr. Masaru Emoto, an esteemed researcher, shared an astonishing discovery. He froze water samples and took photographs of the crystals that formed. He then wrote words on vials of water taken from the same source. The crystals formed in the vials with positive words—such as love and gratitude—were beautiful. However, the vials with negative ones—such as hate and evil—were very different and, in some instances, did not form crystals at all. Other scientists have since done this experiment using various languages, without knowing what the words meant, and found similar results.

What this proved was that thoughts and feelings affect physical reality. As our body is three-quarters water, the implications of this research created an entirely new awareness of the power of the words we use and the stories we tell ourselves about who we are or are not.

Self-blame and criticism keep a lid on our power to create beauty, joy, success, and prosperity. Instead, it creates a block in us that stops us from loving (or sometimes even liking) ourselves and allows very little good to come into our lives.

As a mother, it has been my pattern to berate myself for the many mistakes I made while raising my children. I am now diligent in forgiving myself. It took me a while to remember I started the journey of motherhood as a child myself. I began with no skills other than helping my mom with my siblings. I kept trying to figure it out on my own because in our family, we did not ask for help. And at that time, I knew of no resources available for guidance.

To this day, whenever a memory comes up for me that causes me pain, regret, or suffering, I pause right then and there. Usually, I get onto my yoga mat and say the Ho'oponopono prayer until the feelings subside, and I can raise my vibration into one of love.

Holding onto resentments, blame, or guilt causes an energy leak within ourselves. The good news is letting go of old hurts through forgiveness liberates us to choose love, which opens us up to more joy, love, and abundance. Once we do this, we gain a new perspective on our life stories and retell them in a way that empowers us to create the life we want.

As Maya Angelou said, "Do the best you can until you know better. Then when you know better, do better."

As you continue your journey to becoming your best self, you will keep discovering more of who you are meant to be. There is an impulse within us that urges us toward self-discovery and our unfoldment. We evolve through four stages of awareness that lead to expanded freedom as we grow.

1. "To me" (or why me) stage. In this stage, you feel like life is happening to you by something outside of yourself. It is as though some external force or circumstance controls your destiny, and it causes a feeling of victimhood.

2. "By me." This stage is when you recognize a co-responsibility for your life. You realize that you are responsible for your actions and life as a co-creator with life itself.

3. "Through me." This stage is where it feels like you are in the flow of life—in the zone. For example, you are speaking, and wisdom you didn't know you had pours out of you. Or you are engaged in activities you are passionate about and perform them in a way that exudes a genius quality.

4. "As me." This stage is known as enlightenment. The Buddha is known for his ability to be in this stage, and at this highest level of awareness, he says, "I Am Awake."

My prayer for all of us is to be awake more often than asleep.

Marilyn Rose, one of my clients, had a powerful healing experience when she became aware that she had a pattern of telling herself a victim story when her life was not going well. Recently, she received a diagnosis of terminal lung cancer. Rather than defaulting to an old pattern, she crafted a crystal-clear vision for her life full of love, joy, and travel with her husband. They purchased a motorhome and set out on the adventure of a lifetime. She is combining her gifts of writing, singing inspirational songs, and sharing her journey on her travel blog.

She claims that if she did not have that new vision to focus on and the support of the women in the DreamBuilder Program, she would be living in her dad's basement with her head under the pillows, waiting to die.

Marilyn says, "Today I am focused on healing, growing, living my purpose, and sharing my gift of inspiration. I am focused on living my life to the fullest and inspiring others to do the same. I am focused on inspiring others to find the gifts within all of life's challenges and to live life in a state of GRACE (**G**ratitude, **R**espect, **A**cceptance, **C**ourage & **E**xcitement). And that is a life worth living for!" Marilyn composed and professionally recorded "Dream Building," a theme song for all of the women in the DreamBuilder Program.

Scan the QR Code with your smartphone to hear Marilyn Rose as she sings the Dream Builder song or go to:
https://youtu.be/jItvQFcOawl

No matter where you feel you are on the journey, always celebrate your growth along the way, both the seen and the unseen. Your life begins to change the moment you commit to yourself, even if those changes seem small or insignificant at first. Celebrating yourself creates more success!

Your journey doesn't end with this book. I have developed bonus tools to help keep you focused, empowered, and elevated. They're free and downloadable on my website: www.patriciacampbell.ca

I leave you with one question to ask yourself every day: "What action step can I take *today* to support my continued growth?"

**"Whatever you dream you can do, begin it.
Boldness has genius, power, and magic in it."
—Johann Wolfgang von Goethe**

AND SO DO YOU!

"NEVER EVER GIVE UP!"

Bibliography

Amen, Daniel. *Unleash the Power of the Female Brain*. Harmony Books, 2013.

Bolen, Jean Shinoda. *Close to the Bone*. Scribner, 1998.

Calaprice, Alice. The Ultimate Quotable Einstein. Princeton University Press, 2010.

Collier, Robert. *Secret of the Ages*. TarcherPerigree, 2007.

"Eleanor Roosevelt Quotes." *Goodreads*, 2022. https://www.goodreads.com/quotes/tag/eleanor-roosevelt

Emoto, Masaru. *The Hidden Messages in Water.* Atria Books, 2005

Gawain, Shakti. *Creative Visualization.* Bantam, 1982.

Harper's Bazaar Staff. "21 of Maya Angelou's Best Quotes to Inspire." *Harper's Bazaar*, May 22, 2017. https://www.harpersbazaar.com/culture/features/a9874244/best-maya-angelou-quotes/

Hawkins, David R. *Power vs. Force.* Hay House, 2002.

"Henry Ford Quotes." *Goodreads,* 2022. https://www.goodreads.com/author/quotes/203714.Henry_Ford

Hill, Napoleon. *Think and Grow Rich.* TarcherPerigree, 2016.

Iyengar, BKS. *Light on Life.* Raincoat Books, 2007.

"Joan Baez Quotes." *BrainyQuote*, 2001-2022. https://www.brainyquote.com/authors/joan-baez-quotes

"Johann Wolfgang von Goethe Quotes." *AZ Quotes*, 2022. https://www.azquotes.com/author/5628-Johann_Wolfgang_von_Goethe

Kasanoff, Bruce. "Intuition is the Highest Form of Intelligence." *Forbes*, Feb. 21, 2017. https://www.forbes.com/sites/brucekasanoff/2017/02/21/intuition-is-the-highest-form-of-intelligence/?sh=2e90466e3860

Liles, Maryn. "125 Famous Dalai Lama Quotes to Change Your Life." *Parade*, June 25, 2022. https://parade.com/1247081/marynliles/dalai-lama-quotes/

McCarlane, Paul, and Reuters. Editorial "Nelson Mandela was a Hero who Conquered Bitterness & Hate." *The Globe and Mail*, December 5, 2013.

Maltz, Maxwell. *The Magic Power of Self-Image Psychology*. Gallery Books, 1984.

"Michael Beckwith Quotes." *Quotefancy*, 2022. https://quotefancy.com/michael-beckwith-quotes

Moore, Thomas. *Care of the Soul*. E-book ed., Harper 2016, Kindle Edition.

Morrissey, Mary. "Moving Forward with Confidence." *YouTube*, Mar. 9, 2009. https://www.youtube.com/watch?v=Hp1rp_FoTnI

Morrissey, Mary. DreamBuilder Coaching Program, 2019.

Murray, William Hutchison. *"Quotable Quote." Goodreads*, 2022. https://www.goodreads.com/quotes/1465306

Olenski, Steve. "7 Albert Einstein Quotes." *Oracle Blogs*, May 13, 2022. https://blogs.oracle.com/marketingcloud/post/7-albert-einstein-quotes-and-what-they-mean-for-cmos

Ponder, Catherine. *The Dynamic Laws of Prosperity*. DeVorss Publications, 1962.
---. *The Dynamic Laws of Prosperity*. General Press, 2018.
---. *The Dynamic Laws of Healing*. Parker Publishing, 2003.

Proctor, Bob. [Bob Proctor Live]. "Tweet message." *Twitter*, 2014.

"Ralph Waldo Emerson Quotes." *Quotefancy*, 2022. https://quotefancy.com/ralph-waldo-emerson-quotes

"Rumi Quotes on Gratitude." *AZ Quotes*, 2022. https://www.azquotes.com/author/12768-Rumi

Shojai, Pedram, and Nick Polizzi. *Trauma: Healing Your Past to Find Freedom Now*. Hay House, 2021.

"Thomas A. Edison Quotes." *BrainyQuote,* 2001-2022. https://www.brainyquote.com/authors/thomas-a-edison-quotes

Thoreau, Henry David. *Walden*. Princeton University Press, 2004.

Wattles, Wallace. *A Road to Prosperity*. OK Publishing, 2021.
---. *The Science of Getting Rich*. Create Space Independent Publishing, 2015.

Winfrey, Oprah. Quote of the Day. *Good News Network,* March 14, 2018. https://www.goodnewsnetwork.org/oprah-quote-think-like-a-queen/

About the Author

Patricia Campbell is an award-winning, certified transformational coach, inspiring speaker, best-selling author, and a wildly successful entrepreneur at the forefront of the movement for empowering women.

From a struggling single teenage mom to a self-made millionaire, her extraordinary story of transforming her own life is the inspiration behind her bold mission to teach other women it is possible to create lives they absolutely love! Patricia's determination and resilience have inspired women for over 20 years, helping them break free and build their dreams.

Reaching her breaking point at age 37, Patricia committed to creating the life she dreamed was possible. For the next 30 years, she immersed herself in personal growth and transformation, a journey that led her to study with world-renowned teachers Mary Morrissey, Lisa Nichols, and Dr. Claire Zammit.

She now facilitates programs and workshops for women based on the vast wisdom accumulated over those three decades of dedicated study. Patricia offers a clear, practical, proven blueprint for highly motivated women to become unstoppable. She empowers them to break through invisible obstacles and discover their infinite potential for creating richly fulfilling lives.

Alongside coaching and planning workshops for women, Patricia loves spending time with her family, cuddling with her little rescue dog, T-Bear, and exploring the deeper mysteries of life.

I welcome hearing from you with your questions, success stories, and Amazon reviews of my book, *Never Ever Give Up!*

I invite you to leave a review wherever you have purchased my book!

Connect with me directly.

patricia@patriciacampbell.ca

www.patriciacampbell.ca

Get my FREE eBook: Abundance On Your Own Terms

patriciacampbell.kartra.com/page/on-your-own-terms

I offer free introductory workshops to address all aspects of your life. To attend, please contact me.

Manufactured by Amazon.ca
Bolton, ON

29290262R00092